SUPER SCALING

Systemise, Break Free, and Skyrocket
Your Business to Millions

PRAISE FOR
SUPER SCALING

"Alvin's strengths are clearly in turning businesses into systems. This book is full of practical lessons that will always be applicable to any kind of business."

— Michael Lin
Managing Director and Owner, Auston Institute

"This is the step-by-step manual to scaling up businesses that entrepreneurs need to read in order to prevent making costly mistakes and wasted time."

— Willie Lee
Managing Director, Big 3 Media

"We always hear about new marketing strategies. However, this book is refreshing because it talks about the real topics that aren't covered enough—systems, processes, operations, building and growing a team, and execution."

— Hong Ting Wong
CEO and Co-Founder, 2359 Media

"Most entrepreneurs aren't owners of their businesses; instead they are slaves to their businesses. Alvin shows you how to break free of this once and for all."

— Rio Lim
Entrepreneur and Investor

"Alvin has put together a collection of the most practical steps that you can immediately take action on to increase your business value, revenue, and customers."

— Alan Phua

CEO and Co-Founder, Alchemy Foodtech

"The time and money savings you can learn from this book is astounding. Alvin Poh has held nothing back in sharing the secrets of success in his entrepreneurship journey. The frameworks distilled within this book are timeless and will aid you well in your own business."

— Alvin Huang

CEO, Truegenics

"If you're looking to scale your business through a systematic and logical approach, Alvin has written the perfect book for it. These are the lessons from the business he exited, which he started without needing external funding."

— Yiping Goh

Partner, Quest Ventures

"I've found Alvin's book to be essential for entrepreneurs who are looking to scale up their businesses. If you want to get your business to the next level, you need to read this book now."

— Eric Feng

Social Media Strategist and Global Speaker

SUPER SCALING

Systemise, Break Free, and Skyrocket Your Business to Millions

Alvin Poh

Candid Creation Publishing

First published 2021

Candid Creation Publishing books are available through most major bookstores in Singapore. For bulk order of our books at special quantity discounts, please email us at enquiry@candidcreation.com.

SUPER SCALING
Systemise, Break Free, and Skyrocket Your Business to Millions

Author:	Alvin Poh
Publisher:	Phoon Kok Hwa
Editor:	Patricia Ng
Layout:	Geelyn Lim
Cover design:	Ryanne Ng
Published by:	Candid Creation Publishing LLP
	167 Jalan Bukit Merah
	#05-12 Connection One Tower 4
	Singapore 150167
Website:	www.candidcreation.com
Email:	enquiry@candidcreation.com
Facebook:	www.facebook.com/CandidCreationPublishing
ISBN:	978-981-18-0647-6

Name(s): Poh, Alvin.
Title: Super scaling : systemise, break free, and skyrocket your business to millions / Alvin Poh.
Description: Singapore : Candid Creation Publishing, 2021. | Includes bibliographical references.
Identifier(s): OCN 1249621323 | ISBN 978-981-18-0647-6 (paperback)
Subject(s): LCSH: Entrepreneurship. | Success in business.
Classification: DDC 658.421--dc23

To all the entrepreneurs out there
making the world a better place
through the businesses that they create

CONTENTS

ACKNOWLEDGEMENTS

This book would not be possible without the lessons and experiences that made me the person I am today. As I look upon my entrepreneurship journey, there are many people who have touched my life, and I would like to acknowledge them here. This is by no means an exhaustive list, especially since it spans decades.

First of all, I have to thank my parents and family members for making me the person I've become. If not for the fact that I have tremendously supportive parents, I wouldn't be the person I am today. For that, I'm eternally grateful.

My business partners are the most important people in my life, and whom I trust 100%. These two people have travelled my entrepreneurial journey with me and helped shape the person I am now. Thank you to: Jervis Lee, Vodien; Alvin Huang, Truegenics.

Next is definitely the team of Vodien and Truegenics. It has been an incredible journey and I thank you all for being part of it with me.

Vodien was a business that would have continued to struggle with manpower issues had our business associates not helped us find a solution through the resources that they had in the Philippines. I'd like to especially thank: San Singhania, Lantone Systems; Nagender Rao Chilkuri, Travel Cue Management.

When I went to university, I had a burning desire to see the world and wanted to study abroad. Singapore Management University (SMU) was the only school that had an overseas component. I'd like to thank the Dean of the School of Information Systems then, Steven Miller, who accepted my application and inspired me to make the most of my education in SMU.

I'm grateful that the team at SMU has helped me so much in starting and facilitating my scholarship fund. This has allowed me to impact students and was the genesis of coaching others. This scholarship fund has, in turn, opened many doors that I could not have imagined. I'd like to especially thank: Ho Kwon Ping; Sam Wu; Florence Tan; Wai Leng Chan.

My marketing coaches, to whom my career as an entrepreneurship coach would not have happened. Thank you to: Melvin Soh, X-Factor Marketing; Josiah Tan, X-Factor Marketing.

Thank you to my buddies who have supported me, encouraged me, gave me ideas, and pushed me to do more. Special thanks go to: Clement Wong; Michael Lin, Auston Institute; Rio Lim; Hong Ting Wong, 2359 Media; Willie Lee, Big 3 Media; Derrick Chew, Sight Lines Entertainment; Alan Phua, Alchemy Foodtech; Anna Haotanto, ABZD Capital.

The journey that I took to develop the 5E Scale Engine and coach other entrepreneurs would not be possible without bouncing ideas and getting trusted advice. Thank you: Amanda Zhong, AOS Bath.

The largest acquisition deal that I went through was because of Dreamscape Networks, and they were a partner whom I saw many commonalities together with. Thank you: Mark Evans, CEO of Dreamscape Networks.

Starting a new journey is always difficult. I am greatly honoured and grateful for my first batch of masterclass participants, as well as my first batch of coaching clients. Thank you all for trusting me to bring you further and giving me the confidence to continue with this new segment in my life.

FOREWORD

Asking "why" is a way of thinking that I encourage people to adopt and incorporate in their lives. It's been what drove me to do everything that I did—from civil society, business, education and academia, and journalism—and ultimately created who I am today. This approach of asking "why" about the world is present in many aspects of the book that Alvin has written.

As Alvin has shared in this book, his methodology is made up of five principles: Evolve, Envision, Empower, Engage, Execute. Like other practical books for those who are foolhardy or brave, visionary or ignorant enough—these attributes are the two sides of a coin—to embark on an entrepreneurial journey, Alvin's advice is grounded in business fundamentals and his own experience, and will help light the path along the journey.

With fundamentals, everything must be done for a reason. The clearer we are about what the reason is, the easier it is to set out goals and the easier it is to achieve those goals. Alvin's mission is to help people see these things for themselves and to act on what they see.

We have to remember that businesses are ultimately run by humans. And humans are not robots. That is why developing a company culture that recognises this and grows a high-performing team, rather than a group of individuals, is so important. This is where knowing the "why" is so important.

- Why should your employees work in your business?
- Why is your business a good match for them, in terms of their professional growth?
- Why does your business exist?
- Why should a customer choose your business over someone else's?

My wife, Claire Chiang, and I wanted to bring development to poor parts of Asia and to infuse whatever we did with our values, which were authenticity, being adventurous, the romance of travel, and daring to dream. I had a vision of creating a brand with proud Asian origins. Not necessarily "ethnic" in nature, but strongly Asian in heritage, while being able to incorporate the beauty of the country it is in—be it Thailand, Austria, Cuba, Greece, Mexico, China, or any of the countries that we are in.

This was the vision that kept not just myself, but my entire team, focused on how the business would turn out to be. Through our ups and downs, the organisational vision had to be big enough not just for our shareholders but also be something that excited our employees and customers.

Only after you have a sense of purpose for your team can you expect organisational excellence. I appreciate that this is the last principle of the 5E Scale Engine because I know what it takes before you can expect performance from your team.

Through my business, I've seen how transformational and important good business leadership can be. That aspect of people development is interesting and fascinating to me, because I've been in a position where I've seen how poor company cultures can be toxic and debilitating. In fact, it is our people that drive me and give me a sense of purpose.

As the founding Executive Chairman of Banyan Tree Holdings, an international hospitality business, I appreciate the importance of systems and processes even while one is absorbed by visions and inspirations. Furthermore, as a business that is looking to scale up, systems are paramount. For entrepreneurs, starting and nurturing a growing business is an exciting phase of their business cycle, but they need a different mindset and methodologies to switch into scaling phase.

The 5E Scale Engine has identified the steps that you need to focus on in order to properly systemise and structure your business processes. This book is an essential manual to understand how to scale.

Enjoy the read, and I wish you the very best in scaling up your business.

Ho Kwon Ping
Founder and Executive Chairman
Banyan Tree Holdings

PREFACE

At the age of 33, I sold my internet business for S$30 million.

This was the business that I scaled up from S$0 all the way to be Singapore's #1 hosting provider with 35,000 clients and a team of 150 before the 8-figure exit.

It didn't happen overnight though, nor was it always smooth sailing. Scaling up was a highly turbulent journey that allowed me to learn a lot of lessons and go through a wide range of experiences. This process took seventeen years until the acquisition happened.

After all, I was running this business together with my co-founder, and both of us dove into business as students. We had to figure everything out ourselves, and learn how to survive, grow, and finally scale the business.

A lot of times, we felt like we were spinning our wheels, not getting anywhere. Other times, we felt trapped by the business, as though we were having full-time jobs.

Business definitely didn't feel glamorous or prestigious or comfortable. It was more accurate to say that we were constantly stressed out and our limits were fully tested.

Eventually, we figured how things worked, after solving problem by problem, and making mistake after mistake.

We scaled the business up, becoming the largest market player in Singapore. That attracted the attention of many private equity fund investors and operators from outside of Singapore. One of them was Dreamscape Networks, which was an operator in the same industry as Vodien. Just like how Vodien was the largest in Singapore, they were the largest in Australia and wanted to expand into South East Asia.

Seeing that there was a common vision, we went ahead with the deal and Dreamscape Networks acquired our company wholly in 2017 for S$30 million.

After the acquisition, I had to take stock of my life. The one thing that had occupied my time for half of my life was now gone. I felt lost and without purpose.

In order to clear my mind, I decided to sell all the possessions that I had, so that I could start from a fresh slate. Without anything that was holding me back, I spent the next two years travelling the world and exploring new hobbies like snowboarding, kite-surfing, and many more. I even went to live with Mongolian nomads!

At the end of those two years, I was very grateful that I finally managed to experience all of that. However, the experience only showed me one thing—my true passions lay in business and entrepreneurship. Other hobbies might be a nice distraction from time to time, but I found myself always gravitating back towards business.

In 2020, I returned to Singapore, thankfully before Covid-19 fully struck. I spent months developing and crystallising the knowledge and experiences that I had acquired in my entrepreneurship journey. I wanted to use my skills and experiences to help other entrepreneurs, just like myself, super scale their businesses, so that they can also achieve breakthrough profits and find time freedom.

The way I do this is through my proven methodology that consists of five proven principles—the 5E Scale Engine. This book will walk you through the methodology and show you how I used it to structure and super scale my business.

Chapter 1

HOW IT ALL BEGAN

S$30 million.

Thirty, with six zeroes after it.

That's how much I sold my business for.

It's A LOT of money. Till today, I have to be honest that I still haven't fully comprehended how large that sum is.

If you had asked me when I was fifteen years old if I knew I was going to grow up and run an 8-figure business, I would have thought you were nuts.

I came from a very humble background, where I had to work for my own allowance because my family couldn't afford anything more than money for my lunch in school and my bus fare.

Let me tell you more about my upbringing so that you will have a better idea of how my growing-up years were like.

Growing Up as a Poor Kid

My earliest recollections were of me as a young boy. I grew up in a lower/middle-class family, and I was my parents' eldest child.

My parents were not very highly educated, but when we were children, they gave us all that we needed and ensured that we went through school and got all the education that we required.

Anything more than that though, was difficult. We weren't starving, but we definitely weren't well-to-do. I remember having enough pocket money to have food during recess in school, and for my transportation to school and back home.

However, if I wanted to go out with my friends or buy anything else, I would have to find ways to save money for it.

When I was eight to twelve years old, I remember being really into toys and knick-knacks. Things like country erasers, Gundam figurines, comic books, and Marvel playing cards. Somehow, I had a collector's mentality, and I wanted to collect every single variant and edition there was.

However, buying all these needed money, which I did not have. So I had to find all kinds of ways to get money.

One of the most reliable ways that I found extra cash was due to the clumsiness of my fellow young peers. It was almost inevitable that they'd lose and drop coins which would fall into the shallow drains around the school. When I spotted those coins in the drains, I'd open the drain covers to pick them up. Sometimes I'd even find S$2 bills in there, which boggled my mind because it was such a large sum to me back then.

It was just unfathomable to me that someone could drop S$2 and not frantically go in search of it. When I had S$2, it made me feel rich because I could buy country erasers from the school bookshop for 10 cents each, or a bowl of noodles which was 50 cents at the school canteen.

I'd also noticed that I could make some small change by helping my friends buy things, much like a concierge would. It could be because they couldn't go out to the shops, or that they didn't have time, or that the shops were too far away from them, or that they didn't want to let their parents know.

Whatever the reason, it was a great way for me to help my friends out and earn a little pocket change from a mark-up for my services. I'd help people buy things like books, toys, or music CDs from the shops that I'd pass on my way home.

My First Computer Changed My Life

When I was around fourteen years old, my father got a computer for his work. That changed my life, even though it was just a basic computer that my dad put together. My dad had bought parts from the computer shop and built a computer himself.

I started playing around with the computer, and it fascinated me. When dial-up internet became more prevalent, we got a dial-up modem. I would go online to chat with my friends.

I can still remember vividly how going online was such an experience every single time. Clicking the "Connect to the Internet" button would entail the modem making horrible screeching and beeping noises before you get connected. That wasn't the end of your troubles though. Since the internet was made available through land lines, and my household only had one phone line, I was always in fear of anyone calling our phone number while I was online. If that happened, or if anyone picked up the phone after the connection was established, you would get disconnected! These days, going online is so smooth and seamless.

The primary online chat software that we used back then was mIRC. The cool thing about mIRC was that it allowed you to install "scripts", which were customised themes with added functionality programmed in. These scripts were typically passion projects and were free to download.

When I was toying around with my first few scripts, I found that they were all lacking one thing or another. One day, I got so annoyed that I just told myself that I could come up with a better script.

And so I did. After I made my decision, I spent several weeks figuring it out. It was difficult because I had no prior programming skills, but I dove into the work eagerly because I was so interested in developing it.

This was around 1995. Online documentation and tutorials were scarce, and Google wasn't around yet. We had the first few search engines like Yahoo! and AltaVista, but we didn't have a lot of content creators online, much less video platforms, such as YouTube.

A lot of learning I did was through trial and error, and through reverse-engineering whatever scripts were out there. I spent many nights at the computer, just tediously trying out different combinations of code.

Since I didn't know the language, I felt like a toddler learning a new language. I was learning through a process of trial and error. I tried many variations, and many of them didn't work; but that process gave me a good understanding of how things operated. I followed that process for every feature that I wanted to program into my mIRC script until I found what worked, before moving on to the next feature I wanted.

Finally, after months of development, I made a script that I was proud of, and felt ready to release the first version. However, I realised that I didn't have a name for it.

It turned out that coming up with the name was a big stumbling block for me. I didn't feel very creative and I didn't know what a good name for my script was. So my mind went to my hobbies and the things that I liked. I was a big fan of military helicopters back then, and the Comanche was the name of an attack helicopter that I thought was pretty cool. I decided to call my script "Comanche Script".

When it was ready, I released it on the mIRC script websites for others to download. I also gave it to all my friends. The initial weeks were spent fixing bugs and putting in features that people wanted to see. In fact, I got even busier because now, I had other people to be accountable to. However, I was happy—it was such a joy for me to see others using the script that I had created!

After all that scripting, I had a pretty decent grasp of programming and graphic design. When my relatives knew I was always using computers, one of them approached me to do up a basic website.

I hadn't any experience doing up websites prior to that, but I said yes anyway. Luckily, the project was rather straightforward. I figured how things worked and pieced together a website design. For my efforts, I got paid a token amount.

To the teenager that I was, it was a huge breakthrough! I was happy about my achievement, but more than that, it had also sparked an idea in my head: "If my relative could pay me for this, then theoretically, other people will too."

That was when I decided to put out advertisements about my website design services online. I used all the free websites that were available, and I managed to find a handful of clients from there.

When they found out that I could do a decent job at a good rate, they referred me to their business friends who needed website designs as well.

That was how I got started, and my little side-business grew at a slow, steady pace. At this time, I was 16 years old, and this little business gave me around S$500–S$1,000 every month.

Making My First Major Life Decision

When I was sixteen years old, I made a decision that would change my life forever.

Up to this point, I had listened to and done everything that my parents had told me was good for me. I went to schools that they decided on. I participated in sports, activities, clubs, and organisations that my parents thought I should be in.

However, it didn't change the fact that I hated school. It was made worse by the fact that at 16, I was in Secondary 4 and all my teachers and my parents were forcing me to study hard for the O-level exams.

I told myself that I would do it, just so that I could get it over and done with. I was looking forward to completing it, because I thought life after the O-level exams would be much better.

So I put my mischievous, playful self aside and really studied hard for the exams. Everything took a back seat. I didn't even use the computers as much that year.

To my credit, the hard work paid off, and I did pretty well. I still remember my parents beaming with pride when they saw my results. In fact, it was good enough for me to get into Victoria Junior College, which was a really good school. It definitely felt like I did something right!

However, on the first day that I went there, I realised that I had made a grave mistake. Life wasn't better after the O-levels. In fact, it was worse.

The junior college was just as regimental as my secondary school. On top of that, it was even more competitive. Everyone came in from different secondary schools, but everyone was talking about grades.

I hated it.

What I knew was that I loved programming. I really wanted to pursue my passion in computers. The junior college had a module on computing, but I felt like it was too theoretical and dry. So one day, I started looking around at what other options I had, and I discovered the polytechnics and their diploma courses.

I made time to go down to the open house events that the polytechnics had, and it filled me with excitement. My mind was buzzing with curiosity and the sheer possibilities. I had all these questions about programming and computers, and I was asking a tonne of questions of the lecturers who were staffing the events. I loved the fact that I was talking to lecturers who actually were programmers.

After attending the open houses and doing as much research as I could on the courses available, I finally decided that I wanted to go to Temasek Polytechnic (TP). This was the nearest polytechnic to where I lived, which made it the most convenient option. It had also recently renovated its campus, so was new and had a beautiful view of the reservoir, which attracted me immensely. I made up my mind to take a diploma course there.

Except that there was one problem.

My family wasn't well-to-do. When I was growing up, all that my parents wanted of me was to go to a university because they wanted me to be an educated professional, and not have the life that they had. They felt that a university education would give me the opportunities that they never had.

In fact, at that time, everyone in school seemed to want that path as well. The de facto route was to go to a junior college because you could then take the A-levels, which was a more accepted entry route to universities.

Somehow, despite all these odds against me, I managed to convince my parents. Or perhaps it was because they saw that they couldn't dissuade me! I had prepared all my facts and research about the diploma course that I wanted to take, and I was absolutely confident that I wanted to do this. It definitely helped that I knew I didn't want to remain in a junior college.

Despite my confidence about my choice, I was absolutely scared because I didn't know what was going to happen. I only knew what my passions were, and I knew I didn't want to take the default route of going to a junior college because it was what people accepted as the norm. I'm thankful that my parents supported my decision, and I promised myself that I would do the best I could when I went to TP.

Shortly after, I left Victoria Junior College, and officially matriculated into TP.

It was my first major life decision, and I can say my life changed completely from that point. Especially since the guy I sat down beside during TP's Orientation Day eventually turned out to be my business partner of seventeen years.

How I Met My Business Co-Founder

The first day of school was Orientation Day. I went into the auditorium where everyone was gathered and I sat beside a person whom I had never met before in my life.

We hit it off immediately, and from then on, we were inseparable. The only reason why we would even have been friends was because both of us had a very strong desire to do well in school. Because of this, we stuck together.

We were in the same team for all our school projects, and did really well, oftentimes scoring top of the class. We attributed it to our common work ethic and complementary personalities.

When the school holidays arrived, we started looking for part-time work. We did some work together, but always felt like there was more that we could do. I was still doing web design work on the side and one day, I asked him if he'd like to do it together as a business.

I had some customers and referrals already and we could hit the ground running. The whole premise behind it made total sense to me: If I could make money doing it by myself, then with my friend we could make more by taking on bigger and more projects together.

He thought so too, and was agreeable to my proposal. That was the birth of Vodien.

At the start, we were a web design studio. We designed websites for our customers, and sometimes that included some web programming too. We used PHP as our choice of web programming language because it was widely supported and used.

Being in school at that time turned out to be a great thing! I remember sometimes facing problems with the client projects we had, and immediately being able to get them answered by our lecturer in school the next day.

I felt that my classes were incredibly purposeful and necessary, because almost everything that I learnt had real-world applications!

We ran the business this way for one to two years, juggling school and work. However, when the demands of life started to increase, we were forced to consider a business pivot.

It was then that we thought long and hard about the resources available to us, what we wanted to achieve, our strengths and weaknesses, as well as gaps in the market. Combining these factors led us to land on the business idea of providing web hosting services. After all, the biggest resource that we had were our web design customers.

When you really break it down, all that our customers wanted was to have their own website. There were essentially only two main things that were needed to have your own website: web design and web hosting. Web design is basically how the website looks like, and web hosting is essentially the space on which websites would reside on.

At that point, we had our own website as well, and we also helped our customers with their web hosting services. In order to do that, we had been reselling web hosting services from other businesses. However, it was a difficult process because it meant being at the mercy of whoever we were working with. Sometimes services would go down and we would be stuck between our angry customers and the business we were reselling from.

We knew, first-hand, how it was like to be in our customers' shoes because we were customers of the web hosting industry ourselves. It was clear to us what the problems were, and we were convinced that we had a chance of competing in the space. Knowing that gave us a lot of conviction of our competitive difference—we vowed to create a web hosting company that could fix those issues.

We ploughed whatever profits and personal savings that we made over the years back into the business. With the funds, we bought our initial hardware and paid for infrastructure services, such as colocation services at the data centre.

At this point, I feel that it's important to clarify and provide context. When I say "initial hardware", I mean just one single server. A server is basically an enterprise-grade computer that's supposed to be running 24/7 and serving applications. In our case, the server was used to serve our customers' websites and emails.

At that point of time, we only had enough money for one server costing about S$5,000. Because of how tight our budget was, our plan was to put all our customers on a single server for the first few months.

It's important to note that computers crash and go down all the time. Servers are computers too and were also susceptible to hardware failures. Those few months were truly harrowing times for us. Sleep for that period was uneasy because we were in constant fear knowing that something could go wrong at any time.

Finally, after a few months, we made enough to buy our second server and we could spread out the load. We could not rest easy yet, but we could rest easier.

It wasn't a simple feat to get to this point, but we were relieved because the business pivot had survived its initial few months.

The next stage was figuring out how to grow the business.

Chapter 2

THE 5E SCALE ENGINE

Scaling a business is vastly different from growing a business.

When I first started my business, what was most important was survival and immediate revenue. This is the "launch" stage, and everything is new, foreign, and completely unstructured.

This is the time when you have to be the scrappy entrepreneur. Almost anything goes, as at this stage, cash flow is king, and your foremost concern is for your business to survive the next day. Your annual revenue is probably below 6-figures, and you desperately want to find both stability and growth.

If you get past this stage, you'd need to make some changes. Just like how we grow from a baby to an adolescent to a teenager and to an adult, our business grows as well. In each stage, we have to think and act differently also. When your business gets to 6-figure revenues and you want to reach 7/8-figures, you have to completely change your way of thinking. The mental models that got you to 6-figures will not get you to 7/8-figures.

It took years before I fully grasped what was necessary for scaling a company. It turned out to be something that I really enjoyed, because I loved streamlining and systemising stuff. And that's what scaling up a business requires: making use of leverage. This involves creating systems and efficiency precisely so that you are able to get the ability for leveraged growth, or in other words, scaling.

However, it isn't as simple as just creating systems. My journey has been a rollercoaster of ups and downs where I realised and learnt that the sequence that you do things matter as well. This is why I have specific pillars done in a specific order in the scaling methodology that I use.

With all this knowledge, I created the 5E Scale Engine. It consists of five pillars: Evolve, Envision, Empower, Execute, Engage. It's a proven methodology to scale a business, covering everything from mindset to the exact sequence of systems to create.

I'll be covering these concepts and principles in this book so that you can apply them to your own business and scale it up as well.

One of the first things that you need to understand is the difference between growth and scale. We must prioritise certain things in order to break away from "growth" mode and embrace "scale" mode.

Growth vs Scale

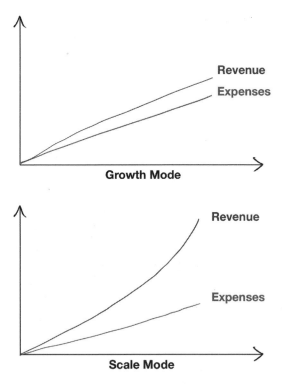

Fig. 1: The graphs depict the ratio between revenue and expenses in a company that is in growth mode (top) and one that is in scale mode (bottom).

It feels like it refers to the same thing—after all, both refer to an increase in size—but there's a key difference between growth and scale. The key difference is the ratio between revenue and expenses (see Fig. 1).

Growth has a tightly constrained ratio between revenue and expenses. That means as revenues rise, expenses rise in tandem.

Growth Companies

That's how you get really big companies doing $10 million in revenue but having $8 million in expenses too, leaving them with just $2 million in gross profits.

In growth companies, revenue is a fancy metric, because when you look at their bottom line, there is comparatively little profit to show.

Scaling breaks this ratio between revenue and expenses. With scale, you see an increase in revenues and, if any, a much-reduced increase in expenses.

Scale Companies

Another company who has also scaled up to $10 million in revenue might only have $4 million in expenses. That means the company has a gross profit of $6 million.

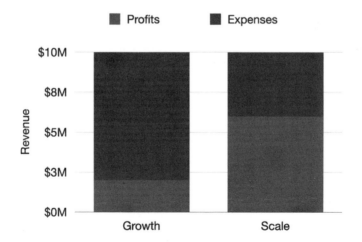

Fig. 2: The proportion of profits and expenses in the revenue received is different for growth companies and scale companies.

In this example, both companies have revenues of $10 million, but their gross profits are vastly different. That's the difference between a business in growth mode and a business in scale mode (see Fig. 2, prevous page).

To be really free of your business so that you can be working on it, instead of working in it, you have to be focused on scaling up your business instead of remaining stuck in growth mode.

Evolving Over Time

It's not necessarily the case that growth is bad. It's just that it's a necessary stage that all businesses need to go through. While being in scaling mode is optimal, it's not something that you can do immediately on Day 1, or Day 500 even.

There are other more important areas that you will need to handle as an entrepreneur. Sometimes all that you need to do when your business is in its infancy is to survive!

Table 1 shows the constraints and focus areas of a business as it progresses over time and through the stages.

	Launch	Growth	Scale
Revenue	5-figures	6/7-figures	8/9-figures
Priority	Clarity of customer demographic and product-market fit	Predictable sales and marketing channels	Systems and holistic customer journey
Focus	Discovery	Survival	Leverage and consistency
Powerful Question	Why should customers choose me?	How do I grow?	How do we scale?
Team Size	0–5	5–20	>20
Hiring Focus	Basic skills (Attitude)	Hire for your weaknesses (Attitude)	Hire for your strengths (Attitude + Aptitude)
Founder's Role	Part-time or experimenting with multiple areas/businesses	All-in, wearing multiple hats and having no free time	Coaching, developing, directing, approving, strategising

Table 1: The constraints and focus areas of a business as it progresses.

The Methodology to Scaling Up

I have personally gone through the process of bringing my business from S$0 to S$30 million. However, my journey was not a straight line between S$0 and S$30 million. In fact, it had a lot of ups and downs and sometimes, I was completely off-track.

Imagine if you wanted to go from your home to your local McDonald's. It should be fairly easy and straightforward for you. Your local McDonald's might even be next door! But that's not how things are like when you are trying to scale up your business. In fact, it is significantly more difficult.

A closer analogy for scaling up is this. Imagine that you are trying to get to a McDonald's, but now you are in a completely foreign land. Oh, and you are also without a phone, GPS, map, compass, or any other tool. You're lost, unfamiliar with your surroundings, without the right tools, and with no one around whom you know. That's pretty much how it felt like trying to scale up a business myself.

I was wasting years making expensive mistakes before I realised how to get unstuck. Eventually, I found my way, and only then was I finally able to scale up my business properly.

I'll show you exactly how I've managed to Super Scale my business, and how you can do so with your own business. I call this methodology the 5E Scale Engine, and it's made up of five pillars: Evolve, Envision, Empower, Engage, Execute.

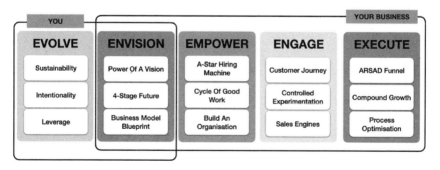

Fig. 3: The 5E Scale Engine.

The 5E Scale Engine (Fig. 3) covers everything from the mindset that you require to the operational systems that you need in order to break free from your daily grind so that you can start systemising and scaling up your business.

Chapter 3

MY SUCCESS WITH SYSTEMS

There's no doubt about it. If you were to ask me what was the single factor that I could attribute to my business being successful, it would be systems.

Don't get me wrong. It's not the ONLY thing that you need to do in order to succeed. However, everything else is a variable and is dependent on your business. What is fundamental and applies to all kinds of businesses is the concept of systems.

I like to think in systems, which helps me get results in a consistent, efficient manner. That is what you need to do in order to get your business to scale up properly.

People tend to think that systems are complex and technological in nature. That's not true though. A system does not have to be complicated nor a technology-based solution. *A system is merely a repeatable set of actions.*

For example, when we were growing our technical support team at Vodien, one of the problems that we faced was that the level of service that our customers would get was not consistent. The quality of service that the customer got depended a lot on who was attending to them.

The solution to this? A system to ensure a baseline of service and support.

So, one thing we did was to create a script that our staff would follow when they picked up a phone call. That removed a lot of inconsistency in the way that our support officers answered calls. That's an example of a very simple system, and you can apply this concept to any kind of work performance that occurs in your business.

It's not easy nor very exciting work, but it's so crucial for an organisation that wants to scale up.

The great thing about the process of coming up with systems is that it allows you to scrutinise the details of a task. As your team documents processes, your team members will be in a position to critically evaluate if any areas need improvement or streamlining.

This is something that I'll cover in much more depth later, as it's a crucial part of the 5E Scale Engine.

Chapter 4

SUPER SCALE WITH SYSTEMS

What can you expect to benefit from with a systems-led thinking about the tasks and responsibilities in your business? The biggest shift is to run your business in a way that you stop putting out fires and start preventing them instead.

First of all, we need to understand why the need for systems. In order to do so, we have to understand what happens when there are no systems. There are ten main reasons why businesses fail (and over 70% of businesses fail in the first ten years of their business life):

1. Failure to connect with their target audience;
2. Failure to deliver value;
3. Failure to track key business metrics;
4. Failure to create marketing and sales funnels;
5. Failure to design a customer journey;
6. Failure to have integrity and morals;
7. Failure to adapt and compete;
8. Failure to control waste and inefficiencies;
9. Failure to strategise and lead effectively;
10. Failure to build a strong company culture.

The good thing is, we can create systems in our businesses in order to avoid these pitfalls completely.

The following are the main benefits, and the beautiful thing is that systems can be implemented for any aspect of your business: operations, sales, marketing, employee training, employee recruitment, and so on.

Understanding Fundamentals

You cannot create effective systems out of thin air. In order to properly systemise, we need to work from the ground up. That means understanding very clearly why we do certain things. This allows us to pinpoint fallacies in our logic and understand why we do the things that we are doing.

Understanding what assumptions we are operating on is one key method. A lot of times we do things subconsciously or unconsciously, so we need to take a step back and understand the bases that we're operating on. Only then are we able to tweak or change it completely so that we can better achieve results.

This gives us insight and clarity, and we can better create a business model and funnels to ensure predictable and consistent growth.

Increasing Consistency

This is the biggest thing that is stopping you from scaling up right now. Businesses who get past the two or three year mark have a decent-enough business model going, because the fact of the matter is that businesses who don't tend to fail and shut down by then.

However, the big thing that needs to be done is keeping things consistent. You will have tonnes of opportunities thrown at you, dozens of marketing campaigns to look at, human resource (HR) issues—be it hiring, firing, training, or anything related to staffing—getting in enough sales, and so on.

Without systems, hoping to achieve consistency is a fool's errand. Systems help to ensure that you hit a level of consistency in your business operations by allowing everyone on your team to follow a clear sequence of steps. In addition, you can monitor and improve on areas that cause failures in consistency.

Implementing Change

Change is a constant. There are no two ways about it. What we can do though, is reduce the amount of change or reduce the impact that change has.

What are some examples of change? For example, if you get hit by a change in industry regulations, and now have to get prospects to agree before you can market to them. Or, like in the case of Covid-19, where it was mandatory for people to work from home instead of in the office.

Systems help us tremendously with this, because of how they make things more predictable. If you have properly documented systems about your workflows and processes, you would have been able to make the leap and have your entire business work from home a lot more smoothly.

If you don't have systems, and if change hits your business, then you will be in a chaotic mess. However, with proper business systems, you are able to localise the effects of change, and even tell what aspects of your business needs to be modified in order to handle the change.

Training Employees

The biggest problem with employee training happens when there are no existing systems. This happens commonly when an entrepreneur hires because he is overwhelmed. Typically, what happens is that the entrepreneur hires someone new to join the team, and then has the employee learn on-the-job or through on-the-spot instruction.

Unfortunately, this doesn't work at all when we're looking to scale up businesses.

I know this very well because I was guilty of that! Instead of relying on osmosis of knowledge, Just-In-Time processes, or ask-your-buddy methodologies, we need to rely on systems. For instance, we need to have a documented set of procedures in order for our new hires to learn how to do their jobs. This gives you a very structured way of training your new hires.

In addition, this also allows your new hires to know what deliverables are expected. You can also have a measurable set of performance indicators so that they can understand their performance and that you can tell their actual progress.

With this, you can begin to unlock valuable business abilities, such as ensuring continuity of the role and upholding the quality standards that you desire.

Making Your Business Sellable

The greatest thing I got from systems was the ability to be working on the business, instead of in the business. This was only possible because of the systems that I implemented within Vodien. What having systems also did was to increase the attractiveness of the business, because it was now a "sellable" business.

The sale of Vodien happened because it was a combination of the right time, with the right buyer, at the right price. However, it would never have happened if our business wasn't "sellable". Here's what I mean. If you are a buyer looking to acquire a company, the following traits are undesirable:

- One-man show;
- Highly dependent on individuals;
- Ad-hoc work;
- Low/no renewals or subscriptions;
- Stagnant/negative growth;
- High employee turnover.

Contrast this with a company with the following traits:

- Organisation;
- Low reliance on individuals;
- Process-driven;
- High renewals or subscriptions;

- Positive, predictable growth;
- Low employee turnover.

The latter is a company that is "sellable". This is because of the focus on systems. Operating a business like this on a day-to-day basis will not be stressful, but fulfilling and fun, because the business is highly systemised.

Know that you don't have to sell your business—many entrepreneurs would rather keep their businesses and run it themselves, and that's totally fine. However, it's another thing to know that you could. Nobody will buy a business that's a one-man operation or a business that's highly dependent on the founder. Even if people did, the valuations will either be low or conditional on the founders staying on to guarantee performance before they get paid.

Measuring Progress

"If you can't measure it, you can't improve it."
— Peter Drucker

This is one of the greatest quotes for business management because it talks about one of the key fundamentals of achieving progress—to know where you are.

If you are a runner and your goal is to run faster, the first thing that you need to do is to establish how fast you're currently running. Then you can measure whether or not your efforts are getting you to run faster.

If you don't measure your running times, how do you know what your progress is? Without measurements, you won't know if your running times are improving, stagnating, or even deteriorating. That's why you invest in systems that help you monitor your running progress—it could be something as simple as getting a cheap digital watch or recording your running times in a paper notebook.

Whatever system you use, you just need to be able to monitor your progress over time so that you can make tweaks in order to get to your goal. This is no different from how you would do it in business.

The following are some examples of metrics that you can use and monitor in your business, across various categories:

- **Sales**: Revenue; Average Order Value (AOV); Renewal Rate; Cost Per Lead (CPL);
- **Finance**: Gross Profit; Operating Profit; Net Profit; Budget Variance;
- **Human Resources**: Hiring Costs; Hiring Time; Training Costs; Employee Turnover Rate;
- **Marketing**: Average Sales Cycle; Life-Time Value (LTV), Customer Acquisition Cost (CAC);
- **Customer Service**: Net Promoter Score (NPS); Number of Complaints; Customer Churn.

Systems in business should allow you to monitor your progress and performance. It makes it clear what your strengths and weaknesses are, once you are monitoring things. This allows you to make tweaks so that your business will be able to improve.

Evolve

"When a flower doesn't bloom, you fix the environment in which it grows, not the flower."
— Alexander den Heijer

This is the first pillar that's necessary in the 5E Scale Engine: EVOLVE.

When I was growing Vodien from growth mode to scale mode, I had to figure out a lot of things. Many of the processes were frustrating me, especially with slow progress and sometimes with progress even in retrograde.

As I came across business problem after business problem, I realised that a lot of the problems had common fundamental issues. For example, I realised that the reason why my team couldn't perform wasn't because of their lack of ability. Rather, it was because I didn't trust them fully, I didn't empower them enough, or I continued to keep certain tasks to myself that I should have released.

That was when I started to realise that I was looking at it wrongly. My realisation was that it had all to do with my own mindset, and it changed the way I went about approaching business problems.

Interestingly enough, the first thing that we need to work on hasn't anything to do with the business itself. In fact, if we try to work on the business, it might cause us bigger issues. The first thing we have to work on is actually ourselves.

Or, more specifically, our mindset.

You have done pretty well to grow your business from Day 1 to where it is currently. However, you need to understand that the mental models that got you here won't get you to 7/8-figures.

That's because as your business evolves, the leadership must evolve as well. In this case, the leader and CEO is you.

The first thing you need to consider is the way you think about things. As a 6-figure CEO, you have most likely been hustling and handling almost all aspects of the business. Most of the things that you do are reactive in nature and YOU do most of the work. Here's what typically goes through the 6-figure CEO's mind: "How do I get this done?"

That's a great work ethic and great mental model. It's the right kind of mental model for you to start a business and grow it to 6-figures.

However, if you want to scale it up from there and start looking at 7/8-figures, then you'll need to change your mental model.

You'll need to think: "How does the business get this done?"

When you think that way, you start thinking about resources. You start looking at collaborations, people, automation, processes, money, systems. Your mindset starts expanding your perspective and vision, and it multiplies your efforts.

The fundamental concept that you have to agree on is this: What got you here, won't get you there.

We have to analyse what you've done, throw away limiting concepts that no longer work for you, and introduce new ones that will work for you.

As the leader of your business, you need to grow if you want your business to grow. Everything that affects you on a personal level must be optimised so that you can perform at your full potential.

Think about the drivers of race cars or the jockeys of race horses. To be the winners in their races, it's not just a matter of the fastest cars or the fastest horses, isn't it?

The Mindset for Scale

To get to and be running a 7/8-figure business will require you to update your mindset as well. So make sure that it evolves, otherwise you'll always be stuck with a 5- or 6-figure business.

The three fundamental mindsets that a 7/8-figure CEO needs to have are:

- Sustainability;
- Intentionality; and
- Leverage.

Chapter 5

SUSTAINABILITY

The reason why sustainability is the key thing that I look out for in everything that I do—be it in my business or personal life—is simple: it works. The fact that you pour years (not weeks) into something will result in you having massive, oversized results.

We see the results of short-term "hacks" in our lives all the time. Years ago, I was interested in the stock market. The ability to trade and have income was very attractive as a broke student. So I did it. I picked up whatever trading knowledge I could from library books and the internet. Then I would start. I used to trade shares with no strategy nor plan. Yes, there would be profitable trades, but there would also be losses. Since there was nothing repeatable about it, it wasn't a system, and it sure wasn't sustainable.

Before long, I was more broke, burnt out, and disillusioned.

Compare this with having an investment thesis and strategy. You wouldn't be fazed by short-term noise or fluctuations because you know what the plan is. If nothing fundamentally changes, you don't need to react unnecessarily. In fact, the best thing to do is not to do anything rash and to just continue on with your original plan.

This is the exact same mindset you need with your business.

That's why I'm never interested in the one-off events and the short-term "hacks". They might bring some impressive results in the near future, but there's a problem. These results are typically not repeatable, so it always feel like a tiring chase than a satisfying reward.

With long-term results, the important thing is to make sure that you can trust and commit to the journey. Since it will be for a longer period of time, you have to be absolutely comfortable and confident in the process.

That's why when I find something that I want to commit to, I find systems to support my journey as soon as I can. I do this because I've come to appreciate that systems create a much more impactful and powerful long-term change, rather than something transient and temporary.

Systems create a structured approach to things, remove the reliance on ad hoc motivation, and avoid the question of "what's next?" when you achieve your goals.

The Problem with Motivation

Motivation is a great tool. It's necessary for us to start doing things.

The problem with motivation is that it isn't reliable and it isn't consistent. We should be thinking of motivation as a fire starter and not as fuel for the fires that we want to build.

We are always full of motivation when we first start something, but this motivation soon dies off.

A great example of this in action is with fad diets. Fad diets are very popular with people trying to lose weight. However, the nature of fad diets makes them unsustainable. Some examples of these are diets that preach for the elimination of an entire food group or for drinking only juice for weeks.

This does result in fat loss or weight loss. People will typically stick to the routine for several weeks or months because they start to see results fast. They power through the necessary short-term sacrifices and use a lot of motivation to do this.

The typical statement that goes through their heads is, "I'm not going to be tempted to eat anything that I really want to eat, and I'll just force myself to drink a juice." A lot of motivation is used in these cases because the person has to actually make a decision to not eat something that is desired and to drink something that is not desired.

That is why when the person stops the fad diet, any weight lost naturally comes right back because the person goes back to his or her original habits.

The weight loss is *unsustainable* because the methods are simply unsustainable.

What's sustainable for weight loss then? To really have a long-term impact on your weight, you will typically need to:

- Understand basic nutrition concepts so that you know what you're consuming and how it affects your weight;
- Identify the unhealthy foods or habits that you can cut out from your life; and
- Intrinsically want a change and the lifestyle choices that come with it.

When you do this, you make changes that are smaller, but are changes that will alter your whole life forever. These habits then become part of a system because you now know what to avoid eating, when to eat, what signs to recognise from your body (is it hunger or is it greed?).

These changes are *sustainable* because the progress towards your goals are offloaded onto a system instead of relying on motivation.

However, systems alone won't work unless you have a direction. Typically, this is done with goals.

Using Systems and Goals

On 20 July 1969, Buzz Aldrin stepped onto the surface of the moon, becoming only the second person in history to do so. Years of preparation and training had preceded that historic moment.

When he returned to Earth, he was an international celebrity. He received the Presidential Medal of Freedom, went on a 45-day international tour, and even had a crater on the moon named after him.

What you might not know is that in the years following his moonwalk, he fell into a pit of depression and alcoholism.

What triggered this collapse?

Aldrin achieved his goal. For a large portion of his life, he had focused huge amounts of time and energy on getting to the moon. Once he achieved his dream, he was aimless. Nothing else could measure up to the glory of walking on the surface of the moon.

Now consider Scott Adams, the creator of the comic "Dilbert". Over the years, he has drawn thousands of comics, written hundreds of blog posts and multiple books, created a podcast, opened two restaurants, and become a highly sought after speaker.

So, what do Buzz Aldrin and Scott Adams have in common? They both highlight the supremacy of systems over goals. Aldrin pursued a goal. Adams relied on systems.

The Problem with Goals

If you've read any books on productivity or success, you've heard about the importance of setting goals. You've read about SMART goals, stretch goals, big goals, inspiring goals, and mini-goals. So here's the question: If goals are the secret to success, why do we fail at them so often? Why do we struggle to lose weight or generate more leads or increase revenue?

Two reasons.

Number 1: Lack of Willpower

Achieving your goals requires constant, sustained willpower over a significant period of time. Whether you're trying to spend less time on social media, creating an employee training plan, or scaling your sales system, you have to consistently say "no".

You have to say "no" to hopping onto Facebook. You have to resist the temptation to chat with co-workers when you should be doing cold outreach. You have to fight the urge to skim the news when you should be working on improving your internal processes.

And the reality is that willpower is not an unlimited resource. Every day, you have a limited amount of it, and the more you use, the less you have. As your willpower is depleted, you have less motivation to work on important goals. You end up feeling discouraged, which further decreases your motivation, and so it goes on. It's a downward cycle.

As Adams notes on his blog:

> *"Going to the gym 3–4 times a week is a goal. And it can be a hard one to accomplish for people who don't enjoy exercise. Exercising 3–4 times a week can feel like punishment—especially if you overdo it because you're impatient to get results. When you associate discomfort with exercise you inadvertently train yourself to stop doing it. Eventually you will find yourself "too busy" to keep up your 3–4 days of exercise. The real reason will be because it just hurts and you don't want to do it anymore. And if you do manage to stay with your goal, you use up your limited supply of willpower."*

The reason it is so hard to achieve your goals is because you don't have an unlimited amount of willpower.

Number 2: The Nature of Goals

One of the odd things about goals is that they are "binary" in nature. In other words, you've either accomplished your goal or you haven't. And unfortunately, you spend almost all your time not having accomplished your goal, which can feel really frustrating.

Adams puts it this way in his book, *How to Fail At Almost Everything and Still Win Big*:

> *"...goal-oriented people exist in a state of nearly continuous failure that they hope will be temporary. That feeling wears on you. In time, it becomes heavy and uncomfortable. It might even drive you out of the game. If you achieve your goal, you celebrate and feel*

terrific, but only until you realise you just lost the thing that gave you purpose and direction. Your options are to feel empty and useless, perhaps enjoying the spoils of your success until they bore you, or set new goals and re-enter the cycle of permanent pre-success failure."

This is exactly what Buzz Aldrin experienced. For a short time after his moonwalk, he was on top of the world. But then reality set in, and he realised that the thing that drove him and gave him purpose was gone.

A big problem with goals is that you don't spend much time celebrating or feeling victorious. Clearly, this isn't an effective strategy.

So what's the solution?

Using Both Goals and Systems

What works is a combination of both. Goals are only effective if they are embedded in systems. A system is a series of actions that you perform on a consistent basis which move you toward a desired outcome.

The way to get more sustainable progress is by developing systems. Systems help define clear routines so that you don't have to rely on motivation anymore.

Goals and Motivation
- Not reliable
- Not consistent
- Not a long-term solution

Goals and Systems
- Reliable
- Consistent
- Long-term solution

Fig. 4: Why goals and systems work while goals and motivation don't.

This is how we scale up businesses as well. We need to find ways to create systems in our businesses so that we don't have to rely on motivation.

Remember, motivation is inconsistent and unreliable (see Fig. 4). Trying to rely on your motivation for a prolonged period of time so that you can reach your goals only results in burnout.

So what is a sustainable system? Remember, a system is simply a collection of repeatable actions. We just need to find a set of repeatable actions that we can commit to doing. In the long run, just by sticking to that system, we will be guaranteed the results that we are looking for.

Sam T. Davies, author of *Directives*, describes systems this way: "Specifically, a system comprises a habit, or a string of habits, that effortlessly nudges you toward the desired outcome." So, for example:

* Goal   — To lose 10 kg.
* System — Go to the gym three times per week.

A good system is made up of relatively simple actions that don't require huge amounts of willpower to do. If you're in the habit of making cold calls first thing every morning, it will soon become an integral part of your day. You won't have to think much about it; you'll just do it.

If something happens and you miss a day, you don't need to beat yourself up. Rather, you can just pick it up again the next day.

As Adams says in his book:

> *"Systems people succeed every time they apply their systems, in the sense that they did what they intended to do. The goals people are fighting the feeling of discouragement at each turn. The systems people are feeling good every time they apply their system. That's a big difference in terms of maintaining your personal energy in the right direction. A system is something you do on a regular basis that increases your odds of happiness in the long run."*

If you want to reach a goal, you need to create a system around that goal. You need to determine what actions you can do on a consistent basis that will constantly move you toward the goal.

So, let's say your goal is to acquire five new customers in the next quarter. Your system could look like this:

- Make three cold calls every morning;
- Go through your CRM (Customer Relationship Management) system every day to ensure leads have been handled; and
- Ask all your existing customers for referrals.

Creating a system like this ensures that you are always moving forward. Rather than feeling like a failure most of the time, you always have a sense of progress.

On top of this, the more you perform these actions, the more momentum you'll gain. You'll start to develop habits that move you toward success. Instead of struggling with distractions and a lack of motivation, you'll find yourself actually wanting to take action. The habits will become so integral to your day that you won't want to skip them.

This was exactly what happened to us when we were figuring out how to grow Vodien. As a couple of broke students, we didn't have the advertising budget to spend. What happened as a result was that we explored all the free marketing techniques that were available.

In our initial years, one of the techniques that I used was cold email outreach. I would try it out whenever I had free time and had a completely random approach to it. This sporadic behaviour would continue for a few months, until I realised that I was getting some results. However, I knew that if I wanted to make it consistent, I had to make some changes.

I decided to explore doing it more frequently. Then I decided to tweak how I approached people. Even though they were cold emails, I wanted to make sure that the email was personalised. So I tried finding the names and emails of their management team, and mentioned clients from their portfolio as well as things about their company's history/background. As a result, it was a very manual and tedious process.

However, it soon became a system. I would have one day a week where I'd spend five hours just searching and emailing these prospects. I would have all the points that I'd look out for in their website, and I'd be able to quickly create a personalised email. And I'd do it every single week without fail. A large part of the emails didn't result in anything, but I managed to find many clients using this method.

Find the 80/20

When creating your systems, look for the 20% of activities that produce 80% of the results. Make sure that those activities are at the heart of your systems. The reality is that not all tasks are created equal. Some tasks produce much bigger results than others, and it's those that you should be focusing on.

Once you've identified your key activities, build your day around them. You need to ensure that your energy matches the task before you. For example, say one of your key activities is writing cold outreach emails, which is a mentally intensive task. You should probably schedule this task early in the day, when your energy is at its highest.

And don't forget to celebrate small wins along the way. Take pleasure in the progress you make. From time to time, look back and appreciate how far you've come. Instead of being discouraged that you haven't made huge amounts of progress, celebrate your incremental improvements.

Choose Your Goals, Build Your Systems

If you want to achieve your biggest goals, you need to create robust systems that will empower you to reach those goals. Long term, sustainable success is the result of repeated actions.

In reality, you'll find that goals are good for planning your progress. What actually helps you make progress are systems. So go ahead and set goals for yourself. But don't stop there. Once you've set your goals, map out what you need to do every day to achieve those goals.

The more you do this, the more success you'll have. You'll experience more motivation, which will lead you to take more action, which will create even more success. It's a vicious cycle.

Set goals. Build systems. Reap the rewards.

Chapter 6

INTENTIONALITY

A problem arises in your business.

What's your first instinct? Probably to fix the problem as quickly as possible and get back to work. But believe it or not, this may not be the best strategy. In fact, going for the quick fix may actually hurt your business.

Here's why. Many small problems are actually symptoms of deeper, more systemic issues. If you don't address the root problem, the small problems will keep coming up.

That's where the 5 Whys technique comes into play. It's an effective method for getting to the root cause of a problem and then addressing the problem thoroughly.

In this chapter, we'll walk you through the 5 Whys and talk about implementing it in your own business.

Ready? Let's get started.

Toyota and the 5 Whys

The 5 Whys technique was developed by Sakichi Toyoda and is used by Toyota.

Taiichi Ohno describes it this way, "The basis of Toyota's scientific approach is to ask why five times whenever we find a problem. ... By repeating why five times, the nature of the problem as well as its solution becomes clear."

In other words, repeatedly asking why something happened allows you to push past superficial reasons and get to the heart of what is really going on. It forces you to look at the problem from a variety of angles so that you can get to the original root cause.

Or, as Edward Hodnett put it, "If you don't ask the right questions, you don't get the right answers. A question asked in the right way often points to its own answer. Asking questions is the ABC of diagnosis. Only the inquiring mind solves problems."

If you want to get the right answer, you need to ask the right questions, and asking, "Why?" at least five times can help you find that answer.

Now, it's important to note that when implementing this technique, you should have the most knowledgeable people regarding the problem involved. They obviously know the most about what might be contributing to the problem and can give the most insight into how to actually solve it.

The 5 Whys in Action

So, what does the 5 Whys technique look like in action? Let's look at an example.

Problem: The shipment did not get to the customer on time.
- Why didn't the shipment arrive on time?
  Because it was sent out too late.
- Why was it sent out too late?
  Because we didn't have all the supplies.
- Why didn't we have all the supplies?
  Because a vendor was late with a delivery.
- Why was the vendor late with delivery?
  Because we didn't submit our order on time.
- Why didn't we submit the order on time?
  Because our ordering software is out of date and didn't properly notify us.

Are you starting to see how the process works? At first glance, it appears that the problem is purely logistical: a shipment being sent out late. However, as you drill further down, you realiae that the root problem is actually the ordering software. If you want to avoid late shipments, you ultimately need to upgrade your vendor ordering software.

When walking through each iteration, always be looking for cause and effect. Ultimately, your goal is to identify a process that either is not working correctly or isn't in place at all. It's not until you find the problematic process that you can really begin fixing the problem.

Now, it should be noted that you don't have to stop at five whys. If necessary, you can continue to dig deeper. However, five iterations is usually enough to get to the bottom of things.

Practising the 5 Whys in Your Company

Now let's talk about how to actually practise the 5 Whys technique in your own company.

Step 1: Assemble A Team

The first step is to assemble a team of people who are involved with and knowledgeable about the problem. It may help to form a team of people from different departments so that they can offer their own unique perspectives.

You also need to include a facilitator who will help keep the team moving forward. Without a facilitator, it's easy to get sidetracked from the main objective. It's important to keep in mind that this really is a team exercise requiring everyone's involvement.

Step 2: Define the Problem

The next step is to clearly define the problem. If possible, come up with a clear, concise statement of the problem, like, "Our most recent product release was delayed by six months."

This step can be challenging if the lines are blurred regarding exactly what the problem is. Work hard to come up with a clear, concrete definition of the problem. It may help to write the problem down on a whiteboard so that you can jot down answers around it.

Step 3: Ask and Answer the First Why

Now it's time to ask, "Why?" for the first time, and find the answer to it. Only accept answers that are clearly rooted in facts. There must not be any guessing or speculation, which can lead you down any number of rabbit trails. Keep everything firmly grounded in reality.

Your goal is to identify the actual problem, not hypothetical problems or causes. Record answers the team provides on the whiteboard so that everyone can see them.

I've found that it greatly helps to identify any assumptions that are present. Sometimes, assumptions cause us to accept the status quo. "That's how it's always been done" is one of the most dangerous and insidious frames of mind for businesses to have. By shifting our lens so that we look at things objectively, it helps us narrow down the right question and answer to focus on.

Step 4: Iterate the Process

Next, go through the above process another four times. Each question should be framed in response to the previous answer. As always, keep things focused and factual. And if the team comes up with multiple reasons a problem happened, that's okay. The reality is that there could be several root causes that need to be addressed.

Step 5: Stop Asking and Start Solving

Eventually, there will come a point when asking, "Why?" doesn't yield any more useful information. At this point, the root problem should be clear and you can begin working on a solution to the root cause of the issue.

One bit of advice. When asking "Why?", you may end up with all kinds of unhelpful complaints and suggestions, instead of the root problem. Always keep the focus on getting to the root of the problem.

Step 6: Monitor Your Progress

Once you've implemented your solution, you need to monitor it to see how effectively it addresses the problem. If the problem isn't solved, you may need to implement a new solution or tweak your existing solution. You may even need to go through the 5 Whys process again to ensure that you've really identified the root problem.

Best Practices

There are a number of best practices that can make the 5 Whys technique even more effective:

- **Focus on processes, not people**
  Your goal is to create processes that work effectively, no matter who is working on them. The root problem is not a person, but a process. For example, if someone's inexperience contributed to an issue, the root problem is lack of thorough training.
- **Avoid jumping to conclusions**
  It's really important to avoid jumping to conclusions. You need to diagnose the problem step by step, without ever jumping ahead.
- **Create an atmosphere of trust**
  When trying to diagnose the problem, people may become defensive or level accusations. This will end up derailing the process. It's essential that there be a sense of trust and openness among everyone.
- **Separate causes and symptoms**
  Work hard to separate symptoms of the problem from the actual causes. If you mistake symptoms for causes, you'll never solve the real problem.
- **Be as precise as possible**
  Vagueness kills the 5 Whys process. When answering questions and diagnosing problems, preciseness is key. Don't accept vague answers.

Arriving at the Real Problems

The 5 Whys is a great tool for cutting through the noise and diagnosing the real problems that plague your business. Yes, it takes some time and effort to work through the process, but it's worth it. Don't settle for surface answers or quick fixes. Take the time to gather your team and ask the hard questions. You won't regret it.

Solving the Real Problems

Now that you know the real problems, the next thing to do is to solve them. The one thing that must be behind every single action and decision that you do is intent.

Everything must be highly intentional. You need to be crystal clear on why anything and everything is done, and done the way it is.

To be clear about my intentions, I use the **Waterfall of Intent** (see Fig. 5) to structure my thought processes.

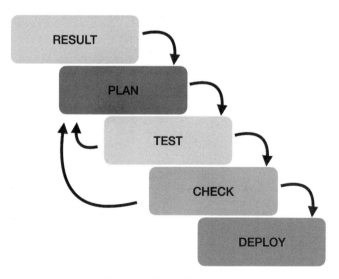

Fig. 5: The Waterfall of Intent.

The Waterfall of Intent consists of the following steps:

- **End Result**

  What is the end result that you want? For example, I want to increase sales from 20 units to 40 units a day.

- **Analyse**

  What is the current state of affairs and what are our current assumptions?

- **Define**

  What new or different methods can be tested?

- **Test**

  Test to see if the implementation works and is resilient.

- **Deploy**

  Make the solution fully production-ready.

Rather than being busy for the sake of being busy, the Waterfall of Intent starts with the results that you want. This mindset shifts you away from just doing busy work and gets you to focus on the goal instead. Be clear on why you're doing everything. Ask yourself if what you're doing brings you closer to your goal and whether there's a better way of doing things.

From the end result, you analyse your situation so that you can define a scope. Then you test it to see if it works, being mindful of whether your actions are bringing you closer to the desired end result.

At this point, you go back to analysing the situation again if your tests fail. Finally, when you find a course of action that works, you deploy all your efforts into it.

Chapter 7

EVOLUTION OF A CEO

This actually applies to any upper management role, especially at the C-level. It's quite natural for the founders to grow together with the company and eventually also pick up C-level positions. So this applies to any of these C-level positions, not just the CEO.

When we are growing a business from the start, we need to be scrappy and be a jack-of-all-trades. Typically, we wouldn't have the resources to hire at this stage, so we would cover a myriad of roles.

That's why we double-hat, triple-hat, and even quadruple-hat (or even more) as entrepreneurs when we're growing our businesses. If you were to draw out your organisational chart at the start, you'd have all these roles in your organisation, and you'd be filling up your name into all of those boxes.

That's not a bad thing though. It's great for a 5/6-figure entrepreneur. In fact, it's required, because the business is still in growth mode, and you won't have the funds nor the capacity to take on a lot of staff yet.

When I started Vodien, my co-founder and I had to handle all the work between the two of us. We were 100% bootstrapped, which meant that we had no external investors. That would be fine if we were wealthy. But because we were poor students, we were running on very little capital. There was simply just no money to hire anyone or even contract out work. If we needed anything done, we had to do it ourselves.

The good thing was that we started out as a service-based business. We provided web design services, so we were essentially trading our time for money.

It was great because we wouldn't have been able to afford the expenditure and investments that a product-based business would have required.

We did many web design projects, which gave us the ability to save up more money. We would eventually invest it into our web hosting business that we pivoted to, which required more capital since we had to purchase hardware.

How to Think as an 8-Figure CEO

It was a tough journey, but we managed to survive through the first few years. I started to look at ways to scale up the business. My goal was for me to be working on the business, instead of working in the business.

That was when I discovered that the entrepreneur's mindset must also grow and evolve as the business grows. This is especially true when you shift to scale mode. You will need to change your mindset to match the new demands of the business, which is completely different from when the business was in growth mode.

When coming across a problem, a 5/6-figure entrepreneur thinks, "How can I solve this?"

A 7/8-figure entrepreneur thinks, "How can we solve this?"

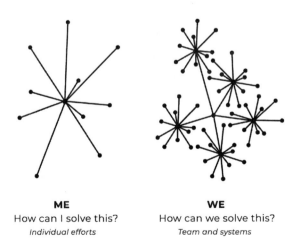

ME
How can I solve this?
Individual efforts

WE
How can we solve this?
Team and systems

Fig. 6: When a problem crops up, the 5/6-figure CEO thinks "me" while the 7/8-figure CEO thinks "we".

Only a single word changed, which is the pronoun "I" to "we" (see Fig. 6). However, the difference that it implies is massive, because you start thinking completely differently.

This mindset shift is where you start to consider leverage and use leverage to get exponentially more done. This involves considering a lot more of two main things in your decision-making process: your team and your systems. When this happens, you are beginning to think in terms of resources available to you, and whether you are able to strategically leverage upon and deploy these resources to get to your business goals.

When you involve your team as much as possible, you start getting them involved in the actual business. Ideally, you want them to be part of the decision-making process and even volunteer to take on the necessary work and projects.

There are many things that stop us from achieving this mindset shift though. The biggest thing that we need to understand and overcome is the Curse of Knowledge, which is what we're going to talk about next.

Chapter 8

THE CURSE OF KNOWLEDGE

When we have too much knowledge about whatever we have to provide, we tend to fall into a trap called the Curse of Knowledge. This is what happens when we wrongfully assume that the other party has the same amount of knowledge about something as we do.

To understand this concept, let's look at a study that Elizabeth Newton performed in 1990. Newton earned her PhD in psychology at Stanford University through an experiment where she studied people playing a simple game.

The game entailed people taking sides as either a "tapper" or a "listener".

The tapper had to pick one song from a listing of twenty-five familiar songs, such as "Happy Birthday to You" and "The Star-Spangled Banner". The tapper would then tap out the rhythm by knocking on a table.

The listener's job was to guess the song, based on the tapping.

Newton found that the listeners weren't able to guess the songs correctly at all. The listeners made only three correct guesses from out of 120 songs tapped out. That's only 2.5%.

What made this worthy of a dissertation in psychology was the difference in perception.

Before the listeners made their guesses, Newton also had the tappers predict the chances of the listeners making a correct guess. The tappers predicted that the listeners had a 50% chance of making the right call.

That's a tremendous difference: a prediction of 50% versus a reality of 2.5%. That means the tappers were off by 95%!

So why were the tappers so off in their predictions? The reason was that the tappers were given knowledge—the song title—and that makes it difficult for them to imagine what it's like not having that knowledge.

In fact, the tappers were oftentimes shocked at how hard a time the listeners had trying to identify the song. Isn't the song obvious? When the listener guessed the wrong song, the expression that the tapper displayed was often one of complete disbelief.

This is the Curse of Knowledge. When the listeners were hearing the taps, they were hearing isolated taps rather than a song. The listener cannot connect the taps the same way that the tapper does because they lack the knowledge that the tapper has.

When we have knowledge of something, it's hard for us to imagine what it's like to not know it. We have been effectively "cursed". by our knowledge. This makes it very difficult to communicate with others, unless we try to recreate our listeners' state of mind.

The Curse of Knowledge plays out each day worldwide, but the tappers/listeners are replaced by everyday people. Every interaction that we have faces this curse, especially when we are running businesses.

As entrepreneurs and business owners communicating to our teams, we tend to use terms that seem very logical to us—terms like "strategic initiatives" or "global leader in ABC (whatever your industry is)".

However, these are highly nuanced terms that can mean anything and also depends a lot on how someone interprets it. It's hard to avoid the Curse of Knowledge—huge information imbalances are everywhere.

As entrepreneurs, we have experience and knowledge about our industry, business, product, or service. The more seasoned we are, the more years we have spent on something, the more knowledge we have. This results in an even greater gap that we have to bridge, in order to communicate with our listeners effectively.

There are only a few ways to combat and overcome the Curse of Knowledge. Here are five ways that can help you build a better approach to communication.

Know Your Audience

Whoever the recipient of your message is, you should find out how familiar they are with the topic that you're talking about. Even if you're a CEO talking about marketing to a marketer, don't assume that the marketer knows all the marketing lingo and concepts that you know. Always check.

Identify Your Assumptions

Whenever we do or say anything, we make certain assumptions. This is just our minds making sense of the world and making things more efficient for us. The key thing to understand is that this efficiency is great for us when we operate alone, but terrible if we want to communicate with others. Whenever we involve others and wish to communicate effectively, we have to identify the assumptions that we are making and see if they need to be addressed in our messaging.

Provide Ideas that are Simple to Understand

The best communicators are not the ones with the most advanced vocabulary, nor are they the ones with the most complex ideas. The best communicators use basic everyday words to communicate simple ideas.

Show, Don't Tell

If you want to communicate effectively, simply telling is terrible. There are too many assumptions that we make when we tell things. Showing is much better. Use diagrams, frameworks, structures, examples, to illustrate your point and bring clarity to your audience.

Get Feedback

The best thing to do is to get feedback for everything that you say. Find out what is it that is unclear. If possible, get your audience to give you the main points about your message in their own words to verify if they've got your message properly.

Knowing that we are all susceptible to the Curse of Knowledge is the first step to improving our communication skills. By keeping these points in mind, we can dramatically improve our communication.

Chapter 9

THE CEO'S
MAIN ROLES

The founding entrepreneur typically transitions to be the CEO of the business. However, this may or may not be a permanent move. One of the things that can happen is that the organisation hires a CEO for the business. In that case, the entrepreneur may take on other roles or may just remain on the board instead.

One good example of a non-CEO founder is Ben Francis, who is the founder and majority shareholder of Gymshark. You may or may not have heard of Gymshark before, but you should find out more about it because it's a modern-day David and Goliath story.

I love its story because Gymshark is a fitness apparel and accessories brand, founded in 2012, that has managed to tremendously outperform the traditional big brands like Nike, Adidas, and Under Armour.

To give you perspective, this is a business that's founded by a twenty-eight-year-old former pizza delivery boy, and in 2020 is valued at more than £1 billion. A large part of the business's success is due to its social media following, and it is significant following. It has over 4.8 million followers on Instagram, and more importantly, has cornered a lot of the fitness influencer market. In fact, influencer marketing was how the brand got popular.

The thing is, Francis wasn't the CEO since a few years ago. Instead, he stepped down from the CEO role and has been Gymshark's Chief Product Officer since 2017. When asked why he hired someone else to come in as CEO, he said succinctly, "You'll need to set your ego aside and ensure the business is always put first, and the people strongest for each role are in those roles."

55

I thought that what Francis did was a great example of what an entrepreneur would do. As an entrepreneur, we need to figure out who would be best in every role in our organisations. Don't be worried if you don't feel that you should be in the CEO's position. Sometimes, we aren't the best people to be the CEOs. Or at least, not for every stage of our business. It could be because of interest, ability, passion, or life commitments. Whatever the reason is, the important thing is to have that realisation because not releasing the role could mean stunting our organisation's potential.

Instead, we should find another role that we can perform better in. Like Francis, maybe it's a role about the product. Or maybe it's marketing, or sales, or technology. Finding what we're passionate about and where we can be performing the best in is another crucial lever for the success of our businesses.

For my journey, my co-founder and I found our callings in the natural progression of things, and how our personalities were. When Vodien grew, we gravitated towards the roles that were best suited for our own strengths and personalities. I became the CEO of Vodien, and my co-founder became the COO, and together we complemented each other and made things work.

Despite having clear roles, it was still apparent to us that running our business was a team effort. The roles only meant clarity over ownership of tasks. We still had many discussions over company-level decisions together.

A CEO Does CEO Work

A lot of entrepreneurs launch their businesses and grow with them. As the founder, they naturally fall into the role of CEO. The problem is that they retain a lot of executional tasks that they have been handling since Day 1 of the business.

One of the things that a lot of entrepreneurs ask is: "I am the CEO, but if I start releasing some of the tasks that I've always been doing to other people in my team, what will I do as CEO then?"

Well, to understand how we can improve this thought process, we need to understand our mindset regarding leadership. For the role of CEO, the top priority is to scale up the business. It isn't easy—I see the CEO role as a big responsibility that comes with major sacrifices that you must bear.

This is primarily because I believe in servant leadership, a movement founded by Robert K. Greenleaf. In servant leadership, the role of a leader is to serve. As opposed to traditional leadership philosophies, a servant leader shares power with his team and focuses on developing people so that they can perform as highly as possible. As such, the CEO role is the greatest servant of the organisation. This runs contrary to what people commonly see the CEO role as, one of privilege and prestige.

The best way I think about leadership is that it changes the default case. If we let things happen by default, or in other words, if we don't do anything, then certain things will happen. However, it typically isn't a desirable set of outcomes for the organisation. Good leadership changes that default case to something that's desirable to the leader and the organisation.

In terms of organisational planning, you must realise that the CEO is likely the highest paid employee. The CEO of a business is typically paid higher, not because of the difference of hours worked as compared to the rest of the team, but the difference of the results that the CEO brings. As such, the CEO's time must not be deployed on low-impact tasks.

This point is tremendously important. It means that if you are the CEO, and if you are spending your time on tasks that anyone else can do, then you are wasting valuable time and resources. It also means that if your time as a CEO is cleared up, and if you aren't doing anything about the scaling up of the company, then you're not doing a good job.

That's why a CEO must be crystal clear about what he needs to work on. One example is to own the business vision. This is a key fundamental responsibility of a CEO. It is why it's also an essential part of the 5E Scale Engine that I teach to entrepreneurs to scale up their businesses.

Owning the business vision means the creation, iteration, and evolution of the vision over time. As you can imagine, this is not something that you can do if you're not living and breathing the business. Nor is it something that you can expect your team to own. This is clearly up to the leader of the organisation to decide on.

Here are ten other critical tasks that the CEO will need to handle. They're similar in the sense that they are all uncomfortable or not easy to handle. They're also tasks that others in the organisation cannot spearhead or initiate.

Depending on the stage of business that you're in, some of these responsibilities might not apply. These responsibilities are very different if you are a 5/6-figure CEO as compared to a 7/8-figure CEO. As a 5/6-figure CEO, you might not have the team, resources, and size to handle some of these responsibilities.

Top Ten CEO Responsibilities

1. **Communicating the vision**
   This isn't a small task. You need to tell everyone about the vision, because people are not mind readers. And it's not just repeating words off a page— you need to communicate the passion behind the vision, and the exciting future that it entails. Do this for everybody, but primarily for both your team and your customers.

2. **Owning the business strategy**
   Businesses are huge, complex beasts. It doesn't help that they exist within an even more complex ecosystem. Your business needs a strategy, and this must be driven by the CEO. You should have the three pillars of a sound business strategy: Near-term, Mid-term, and Long-term.

3. **Be the public face of the company**
   This means taking on all marketing, public relations, and communications. You'll need to be present on all kinds of media that are relevant to your target audience.

4. **Develop strategic partnerships**
   This is something that the CEO is best suited for. You can engage with CEOs and top management of other companies so that you can form partnerships.

THE CEO'S MAIN ROLES 59

5. **Mergers and acquisitions**

Organic growth is good, but don't forget about inorganic growth through mergers and acquisitions. This can be for expanding revenue, acquiring market share, technology, intellectual property, or talent. As the CEO, you should be thinking, considering, and hunting for these deals.

6. **Build systems**

You are the only one in the business who has clear oversight of all departments and functions. Only you can spearhead initiatives and systems and drive the implementation.

7. **Recruit and grow an A-star team**

One of your main roles is to build up a team, because only you know best who and what is needed for the execution of the business strategy. This means overseeing the recruiting, onboarding, training, and progressing your employees so that your goals are met. You shouldn't execute on these but build the systems in place for these processes.

8. **Resolving bottlenecks**

People know that change is a constant. The other constant in businesses is having bottlenecks. With any business, bottlenecks will definitely form within your operations. Once you clear a bottleneck, another one will take its place somewhere else in your business. Department heads can't solve certain bottlenecks, especially if it spans across multiple departments. As CEO, you need to be the one actively putting in resources to resolve these bottlenecks.

9. **Managing and raising capital**

You should have a finance team, but the ultimate oversight of your business's finances should lie with you. That means management of cash flow and large expenses. In addition, if the business requires capital, you will need to be the person raising it.

10. **Developing products**

You founded the business to solve a market gap. That market gap will change, so don't neglect this. Your product and service must evolve with the times and changing customer needs. You might find that you have to create better pricing, better features, or even completely new products or product extensions.

These are the ten critical responsibilities that a CEO must bear, especially since no one else in your team will be able to or can do them. These responsibilities are fundamentally applicable to most businesses. However, depending on the business that you're in, there might even be other tasks that the CEO needs to focus on to scale up the business.

Chapter 10

STOP BEING THE BOTTLENECK

When I was in the midst of scaling up Vodien, I was worried about our growth. We had gotten into 7-figure revenues, and my co-founder and I were starting to feel that we were becoming the bottlenecks of the business, simply because of the number of roles and responsibilities that we were still holding on to.

We could feel that we were the bottlenecks because we knew that so much work was stopping with us. We would be busy every single minute, and we had tremendous backlogs. Most of the conversations our team members had with me were in the form of, "Hey Alvin, did you see my email about XYZ? I sent you an email about it two days ago."

And my response would be invariably either, "Oops, I think I missed it, can you resend it? Thanks."

Or, "Yeah, I did. Give me a while. I'm swamped and will get back to you real soon."

You being busy and overwhelmed may even feel good because you know you're important in the business. After all, if things aren't moving without your attention, you must be important. However, this has dire consequences that affects the business. The consequence of this would be that work would pile up and things wouldn't get done. This leads to subpar business performance, and can even lower your competitiveness in the market.

Start Including Your Team

Over time, my co-founder and I realised that we were terrible business leaders. Not only were we the bottlenecks in our work processes, but we also realised that we were causing our team to be bottlenecks themselves. This was caused by how we were reluctant to reveal certain metrics to the team, such as revenue or sales figures. We were also creating bottlenecks because of the data we didn't want to share with our team.

Ever been a passenger in a car and not know where you are? Or ever heard of the question, "Are we there yet?" There is only one reason why people ask this. Some people think it's because the passenger doesn't know what the destination is—but that's false. Typically, the passenger knows the destination. The child in the back seat knows that the destination is Disneyland, or McDonald's, or the supermarket. The destination isn't the unknown variable. What's unknown is where they currently are. Fundamentally, people want to know this. Even as a passenger, I will bet that you've whipped out your phone before on a car ride, just so that you could check on your current location.

Using our car analogy, not sharing pertinent information is like driving a car full of passengers, but with all your passengers blindfolded and only you being able to see where you are. That's how it feels like working in a business and not knowing what's happening (Fig. 7).

Fig. 7: If you keep things from your team, they are like the passengers in a car
who don't know what's happening.

When we were around twenty-five years old and were trying to grow the business, we were fearful of transparency. We were especially afraid of revealing what we thought were "sensitive" figures, such as our revenue.

This was definitely coming from a mindset and position of scarcity. We were thinking, "Oh no, if we reveal our revenue, everyone will know how we are doing as a company. What if they get jealous? What if they decide to start their own competing business? What if they leave?"

This couldn't be further from the truth. If you believe that as well, that basically means that it'll be true for anyone who is working for a large company, MNC, or listed company. Will people leave, and will some even go and set up their own competing businesses? Yes, for sure. I don't doubt that.

But will not revealing your metrics change that? Nope. The truth is, that will happen anyway. The only way that you can guarantee that from not happening is if you close down and not even bother with running a business.

We found that being transparent and showing pertinent information to our team allows them to understand their individual progress, their team's progress, and the company's progress. This allows them to link their tasks to actual results and see how their role is important in the organisation. This is one of the crucial aspects of developing a team so that your business can scale.

When scaling up your business, one of the other things that you can do is to use the ARSAD method to ruthlessly optimise your efficiency and focus on the tasks that truly bring your business forward. This is a topic that we'll cover in the Execute pillar, later in the book.

Get More Super Scaling Resources

To help you with Super Scaling your business, I've created an online page just for you to access exclusive tools and resources. Scan the QR code on the left or go to:

SuperScaling.com/resources

Envision

"The companies that survive longest are the ones that work out what they uniquely can give to the world—not just growth or money but their excellence, their respect for others, or their ability to make people happy. Some call those things a soul."
— Charles Handy

The second component that forms the 5E Scale Engine is ENVISION.

I never figured out the importance of having a clear vision in a business until after running my business for several years. Thankfully, it was something that my business partner and I unconsciously focused on, because this was what definitely increased our chances of success as entrepreneurs.

It was only after I had the chance to look back and analyse my journey did I understand the answer to this question: "Why and how did my business partner and I manage to work so well together over seventeen years?"

Entrepreneurs and business owners have always been told that marketing is the lifeblood of businesses. Therefore, everyone looks at it as just a cold and ruthless game of numbers. The higher numbers you have, especially in terms of customers and revenue, the better.

Turns out that's not true at all.

Think about it: I can send 100,000 visitors to your ice cream business, but if they are all people who are lactose-intolerant, you're going to find that you're not going to get much, or any, sales (does this remind you of your recent Facebook ad campaigns?).

What's required for a business to work is more than just trying to gun for more customers and revenue. It takes specificity and a holistic approach to your entire business—and to tie all of it together, you need clarity of vision.

I'll show you how the power of a vision can connect you with people that love your message and product/service, and how this will translate into an insane level of results for your business.

You might even be surprised at how common business advice doesn't necessarily work for you.

Chapter 11

THE POWER OF A VISION

As an entrepreneur, we have to visualise a future that others cannot or will not. And this is crucial, because if we do not have a strong idea of the future, then any road will lead us there.

Once we have a good idea of where we want to go, then we won't be distracted by opportunities that could pull us away from what we should be doing. In fact, once we're clear on where we're going towards, we can more confidently say no to the wrong opportunities (and trust me, the wrong opportunities can look so right), and yes to the right opportunities.

Take for example, the seventeen-year working relationship between my co-founder and myself. We worked together from the day we founded the company till seventeen years later when we sold Vodien. Even between the two of us, our working relationship had to be developed deliberately. It wasn't something that developed naturally or by chance. This working relationship was only possible because we were working on a common vision together. However, this vision sure wasn't clear when we were first starting out.

When my co-founder and I first started to grow Vodien, we felt that a vision wasn't important because we thought that our priority was cash flow. We needed to bring in revenue to survive—who had the time to think about vision! However, that was a big mistake.

The problem that I faced at the start when I was starting to work with my co-founder and in a team with my employees, was that I assumed people were mind readers. Or at least, I assumed that what we were doing at Vodien was clear to everyone. After all, if you work at a web hosting company, then it makes sense that you just need to do a good job at web hosting, right?

Well, that's where the nuances are found. Added up, these nuances can lead to a very different result.

After all, what does "a good job at web hosting" mean?

What is "a good job"?

What is "web hosting"?

Is "a good job" represented by having the fastest servers?

Or does "a good job" mean the highest customer support levels?

Is "web hosting" about providing the cheapest web hosting services around?

Or is "web hosting" about providing the most premium experience?

Are we looking at getting the absolute most number of customers, or are we looking at getting fewer customers, but with much higher per-customer revenue?

There were no clear definitions set.

And over the years, I've realised that this wasn't unique to us. Most business leaders, or rather, most people in leadership positions do have a vision in their minds. The problem is communicating that vision clearly.

Being Clear About Your Vision

Clarity of their vision is something that I feel not enough business leaders have. Entrepreneurs do have an idea of the future, however, it typically isn't clearly thought about or communicated well. They think about being a really good marketing agency, or running a few outlets in the city, or having an idea of what revenue they want to hit.

However, that's not a very helpful vision. It's akin to driving and saying that you want to go northwards, instead of saying that you want to head to a specific destination, e.g. a shopping mall or restaurant or whatever it might be. Having an envisioned future is just like that—it means being really detailed about what you're heading towards.

My co-founder and I knew that our focus was for the business to survive and grow. After all, which entrepreneur doesn't? Every entrepreneur would want to increase revenue and get more sales. We were no exception.

However, because we didn't have a very clear and detailed idea of our vision, it led to some very perplexing times. For example, there was a time when we got so confused that we started exploring products that completely made no sense to our overall business strategy. We decided that it was a great idea to offer budget web hosting plans. The idea behind it was simple—people liked products that were more affordable, so that would get us more customers and in turn, more market share and revenue.

It sounded logical, but it turned out to be a complete disaster.

Budget hosting plans attract price-sensitive customers who do not want nor appreciate the things that businesses or enterprises want, such as security, stability, speed, and support. Unfortunately, these things cost money and investments.

When your customers do not appreciate or do not value or cannot afford what you spent in creating your product, then you have a major business model problem.

Thankfully, that mistake was quickly rectified and we didn't lose too much time or money in the process.

The lesson that it taught us was invaluable though. And that is to always know what your business is, in terms of the value that you bring to the table and the target audience that you want to attract.

Don't get me wrong though. There's nothing wrong in providing budget hosting. There are a lot of business models that succeed with that. What was wrong with what we did was confusing the business model and muddling our product type and target audience. We were clearly trying to be a premium web hosting provider because of what we invest in and focus on. And attracting budget hosting customers just meant that it ended up strangling us instead.

Having a clear vision fixes this. Because our vision was vague, we didn't have a clear direction ahead. That affected everything, especially our business model. As a result, we couldn't make sound decisions regarding our product mix and pricing.

Why You Want to Spend Time on a Powerful Vision

I hope you see why having a clear vision isn't just a good-to-have for your business; it's essential. It helps you with the following points too:

- **Dramatically improves your recruitment efforts**

  Your competitors are going to put up generic job descriptions. Your job description will have your vision attached to it. Not only does that attract the right kind of people to you, it repels the wrong kind of people too.

- **Lets you become a confident leader**

  As the CEO or founder, your entire business is looking at you for direction. If you are unclear about your vision or if you start doing things that are conflicting, people are going to waiver in their belief in you.

- **Gets the right people in the right seats**

  The best way to motivate people is not by offering them a cushy job, but by giving them a reason why their role is so necessary. With a clear vision, they can see how they play a part in the business's direction and operations.

- **Reaches out to the right customers, vendors, and partners**

  When you communicate your vision, you're going to be able to attract people. These are people who understand your vision and believe in what you're doing. They would want to either do business with you or want to support you in the vision that you're creating.

  And of course…

- **Allows you to scale up**

  You can't scale up a business if your business doesn't have a solid foundation. A vision sets the entire business on the right direction so that you can handle rapid growth properly.

Anatomy of a Powerful Vision

Coming up with a good vision isn't an art form. On the contrary, it can be broken down into a formula. The only crucial aspect of it is that you need to genuinely believe in it and be passionate about your vision, because you're going to be the one driving it.

A powerful vision is like a road map of the future and is made up of these parts.

Powerful Vision = Core Values + Purpose + Envisioned Future

Core Values

For example, one of Vodien's core values is being customer-centric. That doesn't mean dropping everything for the customer. Rather, it means being empathetic and aware of why we're doing things. This focus gets everyone to better comprehend the customer's perspectives, and to understand that everything that we do in the company is to better the customer experience and to add more value for the customer.

Purpose

This is similar to a mission, but I like "purpose" more because it's a word that I feel embodies the reason you do things. Our purpose at Vodien was: "To enable people to easily launch and confidently scale their businesses online, with unmatched stability, support, security, and speed." I believed with 200% conviction that this was the reason why Vodien had to exist, otherwise there was no difference between Vodien and any other hosting provider. What is your business's purpose?

Envisioned Future

The difference between a good envisioned future and a bad one is in the details and the size of it. A good envisioned future should be huge, and much larger than your business currently is. This is important because it forces you to think differently.

In terms of details, make sure you fully flesh out your vision, with no details spared. If you're providing a product or service, think about how big your company will be in terms of revenue, number of employees, countries served, and so on.

Your envisioned future must be achievable in a matter of years, preferably around 5–7 years, but also should be scary in the sense of its risk and size. It should be clear and compelling and must definitely expand what your business capabilities currently are. Your vision must also bring your business further from where it is currently at and be measurable so that you can see your progress.

But most importantly—never let your vision be something that isn't you. Connect it to who you are: your passions, what shaped you, what you want to right in the world, and so on. It needs to be something that you can be really passionate about.

Here's what Bill Gates said about his vision of Microsoft (Liang):

> *"When Paul Allen and I started Microsoft over thirty years ago, we had big dreams about software. We had dreams about the impact it could have. We talked about a computer on every desk and in every home.*
>
> *It's been amazing to see so much of that dream become a reality and touch so many lives. I never imagined what an incredible and important company would spring from those original ideas."*

Similarly, when Amazon.com launched in 1995, it was with the mission "to be Earth's most customer-centric company, where customers can find and discover anything they might want to buy online, and endeavours to offer its customers the lowest possible prices."

Of course, Amazon is a completely different company right now. It doesn't just serve end-user customers, but has partners, Amazon Web Services, content creators, developers, and so on. However, Jeff Bezos definitely managed to bring his original vision to reality.

Is there a right way to create a vision? No. There are a few things that you should avoid doing, which I'll cover right after this, but there isn't a "correct way" to do this. The most important is to have a vision that you feel passionate about, and to start with version 1 of your vision. I can guarantee that this vision will evolve as you and your business grows.

Vodien's vision started off really small. As a couple of broke students, my co-founder and I had very small visions. In our initial years, I think it could have been summarised as "To survive to the next month" or "To make enough money to pay for our food and transport".

As we grew, we became much clearer in our vision. The vision that we had eventually became: "Vodien is a leading cloud hosting provider in Asia, and prides itself on offering the highest levels of speed, stability, security, and support to its customers."

Its clients included celebrities, private companies, financial institutions, and various Singapore government organisations.

Similarly, you need a strong vision that you will be genuinely excited for. My vision for the Super Scaling Tribe is this:

> *"We are a close-knit community of the next generation of 8/9-figure entrepreneurs who are action-takers, open-minded, and hungry for success.*
>
> *Everyone has his or her network, strengths, and specialisations. We are openly sharing and helping each other because as all of us grow individually, the community grows even more and everyone benefits."*

Notice that it is written in the present tense. This is crucial. Look at how it sounds like when it's written in the future tense:

> *"We will be a close-knit community of the next generation of 8/9-figure entrepreneurs who are action-takers, open-minded, and hungry for success.*
>
> *Everyone will have his or her network, strengths, and specialisations. We will openly share and help each other because as all of us grow individually, the community will grow even more and everyone will benefit."*

Different, isn't it? Writing it in the present tense just makes it feel like it's *already happening*, whereas writing it in the future tense makes it just sound like a wish or hope. I personally find writing my vision in the present tense a lot more powerful.

The more specific you can be about your vision, the better! Think about all aspects of your business, such as:

- What services and products are you providing?
- Who is the customer that you are serving?
- What is the number of customers that you are serving?
- How are you different from your competitors?
- What is the media saying about you?
- What is the amount of revenue that you are collecting every year?
- What geographies are you present in?
- How big of a team do you have?
- What are the departments and roles that your team is handling?
- What responsibilities are you handling on a daily basis?
- Are you bootstrapped or do you have external investments?
- If you have investors, how are they like and who are they?

How to Come Up With a Powerful Vision

If we do what we've always been doing, then it isn't very surprising if we aren't getting different results.

To come up with a powerful vision, I find that the visualising needs to be done outside of your typical routine and environment.

Let your mind be free and wander. If it is busy handling the present—for example, daily concerns of the business and of life—it is hard to think about the future.

Take time away from the office, go to a favourite place of yours where you won't be disturbed or distracted. Don't even type it into your phone or computer. Use pen and paper so that you can really tap into the magic of your creativity.

When actually writing down your vision, never think about "how". Just think about what you feel the future should be like. We can figure the "how" later, so put down any and every single crazy thought you might have.

Okay, You Have a Vision. What's Next?

Once you have a powerful vision, your job doesn't end there. Now, you have to make sure that it's something that burns in the mind of your team. You have to firstly convince them of it, and then always be reminding them of it. That means constantly communicating this so that everyone eventually gets familiar with it.

Don't mistake this as a boring, logical presentation of facts. Communicating your vision should appeal to people's emotions. They should feel and understand the reason for the vision on an emotional level.

I communicated Vodien's vision by tying any efforts and work done in the business to the vision. Everything in Vodien is for one or more of the four pillars that we stand for, in order to give our customers a good web hosting experience: Speed, Security, Stability, and Support. Everyone is super clear about why they're doing the work that they do, and how it all contributes to the vision.

If a customer support officer has done a good job and received a testimonial from a customer, I highlight and mention that in our company emails, knowledge base, meetings, or have some form of recognition for that.

Similarly, if we develop new speed improvements for our servers or software, I make sure it's also mentioned somehow or somewhere, and tie it back to why it's essential for our company's vision.

This constantly reinforces the vision, while showing your team what actions and activities are useful and helpful to bringing the vision to reality.

More importantly, you need to give your team the freedom to create the "how". Your vision tells everyone the "what". Don't micromanage, but involve everyone instead. The way I encourage high performance from everyone on my team is through the Cycle Of Good Work. This increases ownership, encourages suggestions, allows for failure, and creates an environment for everyone's best work.

This is something that I will cover in the next principle of the 5E Scale Engine: EMPOWER.

Chapter 12

DO NOT SET THE WRONG VISION

While setting a vision is great, you have to make sure that you don't set the wrong vision too. When you grow your team, a strong vision will be essential to bond everyone around and provide motivation.

Here are four signs that you have set the wrong vision.

It's Too Small

> *"Shoot for the moon. Even if you miss,*
> *you'll land among the stars."*
> *— Norman Vincent Peale*

How big you want to scale is entirely up to you. There's no right or wrong. However, the only problem is thinking too small when you really desire a vision that's bigger. You will know when you really have a vision that's much too small when it's achievable in a very short amount of time. In that case, it becomes a goal rather than a vision.

When I was in secondary school and going for the GCE "O" Level examinations, I created a personal vision for myself where I wanted to ace the exam and get good results. The only reason why I wanted to do that was because my parents said that doing well in exams was a necessary thing. I had no idea why good grades were necessary or what my future career path would be or how my results will affect my future.

As a result, I set a vision to do well in the exams at the end of that year. I did study hard for those months and in the end, I did do well enough in the exams. However, I felt lost, disillusioned, and unfulfilled right after I got my exam results and discovered that I had achieved my vision.

There was literally a big gap in my life because I was now without a vision and purpose. If I had a bigger vision where I saw how the exam was but a milestone, then I'd have seen that it's just a step forward in my overall journey and would still have had the motivation to continue.

When designing a vision for your business, you need to make sure that it's big enough to span 5–7 years of effort. It needs to push you and your team and guide your decision over those years. It could be big enough that it even seems crazy or ridiculous, especially if no one has done it before. That is a good sign!

No One is Excited About It

You want a vision that is not just big, but also strikes at the emotions of your team members.

This is a pretty big vision: "We want to make $500 million in five years!" However, without specifics, details, and a purpose, it becomes very unappealing. When it's unappealing, it doesn't get your team excited and talking about the vision.

A vision becomes stronger when you tie in a purpose. It could be for a social cause, or it could be something that drives the business more than just profits and revenue. For Vodien, we were very clear that we didn't want to be the biggest just for the sake of being the biggest. Nor were we prioritising profits and revenue for the sake of financial performance.

We had a very strong purpose and that was to serve our customers. My co-founder and I were innately familiar with the problems of the industry. This happened because we were literally customers of our industry before we started

Vodien and, in fact, that was one of the reasons why we started Vodien in the first place.

What this gave us, though, was crystal clarity about how to provide a great web hosting experience. We believed 100% that the single sole reason why Vodien existed was because our customers all relied and trusted us to take care of their websites and email services, and everyone in our team knew that to be part of our company's purpose, or our "why".

It's Not Specific

What does specificity mean? When I talk about specificity, it's about how quantifiable your vision is. When your vision is vague, it's hard to quantify success. The more specific you are, the greater the chances of success.

I made the mistake of defining Vodien's vision to be the "largest web hosting provider" before. I realised that's not ideal, because is it in terms of customer accounts? Domain names? Revenue? When we defined it by total domain names, it was a lot clearer. The entire team could tell when we were making progress, because domain name count was a specific measurement.

When your vision is specific, everything becomes black and white. Either you achieve it, or not. This removes room for interpretation and confusion.

There's No Risk

Risk drives us because of the uncertainty and the pressure to perform. If we pursue something certain or something that has certain outcomes, it becomes boring and unexciting. The right vision will push you out of your comfort zone and make you feel uncomfortable.

A vision with a good amount of risk will result in there being several or many factors that are unknown and outside of your control. In a vision that's exciting and big enough, you would only be able to see and predict a few factors, not all of them nor a majority of them.

That is why movies and stories with risk enchant and intrigue us. I love watching Batman movies because I know he's a flawed superhero. Nothing is certain because he's human after all, and he faces a huge amount of risk and uncertainty every time he faces off with a villain.

Chapter 13

4-STAGE FUTURE

*"It is not enough to do your best; you must know
what to do, and then do your best."*
— W. Edwards Deming

Your goal as an entrepreneur is to flesh out the vision, make sure that everyone is crystal clear of the vision, in addition to making sure the right people are in the right roles to create that vision.

To do this requires good communication. In fact, good communication is something that is often said to be a key requirement of high-performing teams. However, discovering how to have good communication isn't very well understood nor implemented.

The first thing that needs to be done is within ourselves. We have to see if we can clearly understand our vision ourselves, and logically understand what it takes to get there.

When I was scaling up Vodien, the difficulty that I faced was not just having a vision, but understanding how to get there. After all, it's relatively easy to have a big vision, but it's harder to know what it is that we can do today, in order to get us working towards that vision. Once I had a clear idea of that, I had to get my team on board and clearly understand what needed to be done.

The one thing that really worked for me was to have a road map that translated my vision into something that I clearly understood, and that I could use to communicate to others. I call this the 4-Stage Future.

Planning Your 4-Stage Future

Like a map that shows you how to get to your destination, I've found that you need to be able to paint your journey to your vision as well. This is a core function of the 4-Stage Future, as the four stages are all based on time periods.

The first is to know what your vision is. This is the overall destination. Once we have the vision, we can then ask what we need to accomplish in the long term, so that we can actually get there. The key is to understand how to do this logically.

For example, if our vision is to be a popular travel blogger, then perhaps we should focus on increasing our content, profile, and reputation. A long-term milestone could be to attract global sponsorships, but we can't get there the next day. We need to figure out how to make that possible, and what it takes today, in order to eventually get us there.

In the mid-term, perhaps we can focus on smaller, local sponsorships first. In order to get there, we need to know what we can do in this quarter that will move us towards our goals. Perhaps what we could do in the next few quarters of the year is to work on coming up with one travel video every week and reach out to four brands for a collaboration every month.

When we break down a vision into the 4-Stage Future (Fig. 8), then it makes us and our team feel like the big, scary vision becomes logical and eventually achievable.

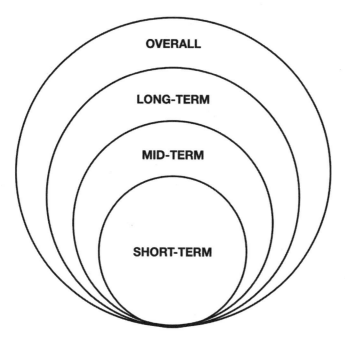

Fig. 8: The 4-Stage Future is based on time periods and allows you and the team to break down a vision into what seems achievable.

These are the four stages that we should be addressing, and their time-frames:

1. Overall Vision (5–7 years)
2. Long-term goal (3 years)
3. Mid-term goal (1 year)
4. Short-term goal (3 months)

Each of these stages requires you to strategise so that you can get to the preceding stage. For example:

1. Overall Stage: The brand that small businesses in Singapore think of when they need to host their website and emails.
2. Long-term Stage: Rise to #3 in market position because of increases in search engine position, affiliate sales, and organic growth.
3. Mid-term Stage: Increase affiliate sales to be 15% of total revenue.
4. Short-term Stage: Find fifteen affiliates who will promote our product.

To help us get clarity and establish better strategies, we can ask ourselves these two questions:

1. What is the one task that, once done, will get me closer to my goal?
2. How do I know if the goal is met?

Once your vision is broken down into the four logical time periods, the 4-Stage Future should clearly show you how to achieve the two main goals of clarity and focus.

Clarity

What needs to be done, today, in order to get us to where we want to go? We need to know this in order for us to move towards a vision. Not only do we need to know this ourselves, we need to be able to communicate this simply and clearly, so that our team can also understand what needs to be done.

Focus

What are your priorities? The thing about entrepreneurs is not that we don't have enough to do. Oftentimes, we have too much to do. It's a matter of reduction, not addition. When we have clarity of focus, we can then start working on the right things.

Remember, in coming up with your 4-Stage Future, simplicity is your friend.

Michelangelo was one of the greatest artists that ever lived. In 1501, Michelangelo was commissioned to produce a statue of the biblical David out of an eighteen-foot-tall block of marble. This block of marble was so inferior that many other artists, including the famous Leonardo da Vinci, regarded it as unworkable. It was no easy feat, and it took the talented Michelangelo four years before it was finally completed. Till today, Michelangelo's statue of David is known as one of the greatest sculptures of all time.

When asked by the pope about how he found the genius to sculpt something like that, Michelangelo simply responded by saying, "It's simple. I just remove everything that is not David."

Keep it simple, my friends.

Chapter 14

WHAT IS YOUR BUSINESS MODEL?

The true nature of the product or service that you're offering isn't about its features.

I came across this interesting story a few years back, and the message I got from it still sticks with me to this day. Anyone who wants to look at business and sales in a new and unique light should listen to this concept about reaching out to possible customers. Maybe you'll even shift your business's messaging after reading this.

The story begins with my family having a gathering at my aunt's home. My aunt and I were having a chat, and she was talking about a vacuum cleaner salesman who came by not long ago. "I heard that my next-door neighbour just spent S$1,500 on a vacuum cleaner," my aunt said. "I can't believe she fell for it! There's no way the salesman would sell me one of those overpriced bulky things."

But three days later, that vacuum cleaner salesman knocked on my aunt's door and ended up selling her that same vacuum cleaner. My aunt even went so far as to buy the special edition with some extra features for an additional S$400.

You might assume that my aunt bought something she did not want, or that the salesman cheated her into buying that vacuum cleaner. But it turns out that things panned out a bit differently.

If the salesman had walked to my aunt's door and directly asked her if she wanted to buy a vacuum cleaner, I'm pretty sure my aunt would have said "NO" right away. But the salesman was smarter; he did the complete opposite of a hard sell, and my aunt was definitely not scammed into this.

The first thing that the smart salesman did was to understand this: My aunt was not in the market for an overpriced bulky vacuum cleaner, but she was in the market for other things. One of which was taking care of the health of her family, herself included.

The salesman had opened the conversation asking about the environment and the dust levels in the house. My aunt had big problems with that, and because she had four people in the family and three bedrooms, there was a lot of space for dust to gather. My aunt talked for an hour about how bad the dust could get. It turned out that my uncle would get bad allergy attacks, with a runny nose and teary eyes, and nothing that they did would make it better.

The salesman listened attentively to my aunt lament about the problems that she was facing, and when she was done going through all of them, the salesman said, "What's needed, then, is some way to clean the house so that everyone can be healthy and comfortable, right?"

Then the salesman made his pitch. The vacuum cleaner wasn't just an overpriced bulky thing anymore; it was an effective cost-efficient solution to the dust problems that my aunt was facing.

Not surprisingly, the salesman got the order.

Did my aunt get conned into buying something that she didn't need? Hardly. She didn't need an overpriced bulky thing—and she didn't buy one. What she bought was a solution to all the health problems that her family was facing.

So there are a few lessons from this story:

Do as much research as possible on your prospect. You have to understand their pains, desires, and motivations.

Make sure you completely understand your product and its abilities. You need to tailor the benefits that it can have to the needs that your customers have.

So, in other words:

- You're not selling Facebook ad space; you're offering a way for a business to get qualified prospects.
- You're not selling web design services; you're offering a way for a business to get online so that they can increase their reach.

- You're not selling washing machines;\ you're offering a way to have clean laundry easily and effectively.

Business Model Blueprint

To help us understand our business model better, we need a structure and framework. The **4WH Business Model** (Fig. 9) consists of the fundamental questions that your business model must answer.

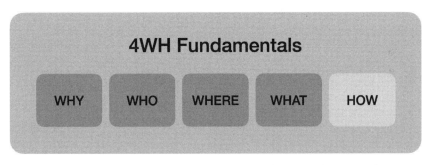

Fig. 9: The 4WH Business Model consists of the five fundamental questions that your business model must answer.

Why   Your vision
           Example: To be the brand that small businesses in Singapore think of when they need to host their website and emails.

Who   Ideal customer
           Example: Small businesses in Singapore

Where Marketing channels
           Example: Google search engine results, Facebook, LinkedIn, affiliates

What   Solution
           Example: Full-service web hosting

How	Costs, pricing, and fulfilment of your product/service
	Example: This is where I figure out the pricing of the products (whether it's premium/budget, how much margin to command, etc), and how to actually set up the infrastructure so that I can start selling to my customers.

Get More Super Scaling Resources

To help you with Super Scaling your business, I've created an online page just for you to access exclusive tools and resources. Scan the QR code on the left or go to:

SuperScaling.com/resources

Empower

"Teamwork is the ability to work together toward a common vision. The ability to direct individual accomplishments toward organisational objectives. It is the fuel that allows common people to attain uncommon results."
— Andrew Carnegie

When I first started hiring team members in Vodien, I thought it was a fairly straightforward process. After all, if I was hiring someone to join a web hosting company, shouldn't it be clear that they need to do a good job at web hosting, whatever their exact role might be?

I thought that all that was required was to put up a job advertisement letting people know that we were a web hosting company and we needed people to join us.

Well, the reality is that things aren't that straightforward.

I was assuming people could read my mind, and that honestly doesn't ever happen. Hiring is all about people. Whenever you interact with people, you'd notice that communications is paramount. Two of the first questions to answer is:

- How should we communicate?
- What do we communicate?

By focusing on the answers to those questions, we can start building up a team effectively. I found out the hard way how to do it by making mistakes over my entrepreneurship journey. In this chapter, I'm going to show you how I overcame it so that you don't have to make the mistakes that I did.

The difference between a group and a team might not seem big, but it can literally mean the success or failure of your business. A group is a collection of individuals with their own agenda, whereas a team is a collection of individuals with a shared common purpose.

The goal is to build up a highly-effective team, because then you can amplify your personal efforts. Herb Kelleher, the former CEO and chairman of Southwest Airlines, realised this:

> "I realised that if you take care of the employees, they will be happy and thereby take care of the customers. And when the customers are happy, they come back. And when they come back, that makes the shareholders happy. That's what the best companies do."

A high-performing team can really EMPOWER your business to achieve great heights.

Chapter 15

BUILD AN ORGANISATION

An organisation isn't an organisation if it's made up of one person—just yourself. An organisation is also not a cluster of individuals.

An organisation is a team, where everyone is working together towards common organisational objectives.

When businesses start, they tend to be small. As entrepreneurs at this stage, we typically wear multiple hats and play multiple roles. It's not wrong. In fact, it's necessary to do this in order to handle the work needed to grow the business.

However, in order to scale, your goal as an entrepreneur is to replace yourself.

This is not a quick process and will take you a lot of time and effort before it happens. Having it happen in months would be very optimistic. I'd say it might take you about two to seven years, depending on where you are in your business currently.

It was around the fourth year of Vodien that my co-founder and I sat down one day and decided to draw out our organisational chart. We didn't and hadn't done it earlier before, because it was just the two of us handling everything.

We thought that we didn't even need an organisational chart even after hiring our first few employees.

However, I realised that I was thinking about it wrong. I had thought that the organisational chart was all about the people. Later, when we were much bigger, I realised that the organisational chart gave me a very good overview of not just the people that I have in my team, but also the roles that I needed to fill. This could have been something that I would have benefitted from when Vodien was much younger and smaller.

Even if you are a small team, I urge you to take time to come up with your organisational chart. However, don't just create it based on your current team. Instead, create an organisational chart based on the roles and departments that you need to have.

For example, when my co-founder and I first started Vodien, our organisation charts would only consist of two names—my co-founder's and my own. That's not important though. What's more important is that we should also be drawing out all the roles that the both of us were playing.

This simple exercise will make things a lot clearer about what roles were crucial to the business and what roles everyone in the business was spending their time on.

Chapter 16

GET A TEAM OF A-PLAYERS

Having a team of A-players is every entrepreneur's dream. However, a lot of entrepreneurs face serious difficulties getting this team. While it isn't easy, actually getting such a team isn't just a pipe dream. On the contrary, it can be quite simple if you know what to focus on.

The first is hiring properly with a system. Most entrepreneurs that I know go through this process of hiring haphazardly. That's not uncommon though—it's exactly how I did it at the start too. In fact, when I was first starting to hire people, I remember that my hiring system was just to go and copy whatever other companies were doing.

That's a big mistake.

Just like how every individual is different, every company is different too. And here's the big secret behind hiring A-players: What I think is an A-player is different from what you think an A-player is.

To make that more complex, it doesn't just depend on the entrepreneur. Each role in a business will have a different definition of what an A-player is. So a sales role in your company will be looking for different things in a candidate than what a marketing role would be looking for.

This is one of the reasons why hiring can be so complex. Nevertheless, we can still boil this down to the essential things that we're looking for. Once we know what these things are, we can then start crafting a set of processes and systems to help us in our hiring journey.

What Does a Simple Hiring System Look Like?

Like any other part of your business, you can create systems for hiring and growing talent. Here is an overview of the steps that you'll need to cover in your hiring system:

1. **Define what an A-player is**

   This is highly dependent on the role and business. What you require and think is an A-player is not what someone else might agree with. In fact, even within your own business, the definition of an A-player will differ from role to role.

2. **Create a job description**

   A solid job description can't be something that you just copy from another company's job advertisement. You need to flesh it out with what your company's vision is, what values are important to you, and what responsibilities the person must have.

3. **Test for the right attributes**

   Hiring is not all about simple, straightforward tests that you have to fill up. Sometimes it can vary, depending on what you think an A-player is. If you want somebody that can respond to customer support inquiries well, then test for it.

   The best way to test for something like that is a situational or problem test. I actually give candidates a real-world customer support inquiry and see how they respond to it.

   In fact, sometimes I even have tests in the job description so that I weed out people who aren't serious, who aren't diligent enough, or who aren't detail-oriented enough. A simple example would be to have them email their application with a very specific filename format.

4. **Have a thorough onboarding process**

Imagine going to a foreign country for the first time, all alone. That's pretty much how it feels like for someone joining your company. The onboarding process should make the experience welcoming and also be structured so that your new hire will know exactly:

- What's required of the job;
- Where/how to get training;
- What your company policies are (i.e. processes for taking leave, code of conduct, etc); and
- Remuneration and benefits.

5. **Evaluation**

Next up is evaluating whether or not the employee is hitting KPIs and is aligned with your company culture. This step is crucial because as much as you can test for attributes and core values in your job interviews, it's still just a test. The important thing is how the new employee is like when actually working in your team.

I've found that there's really no way to guarantee this except with an airtight evaluation period. In Singapore, we know this as the probationary period. The evaluation period is typically three months but can be extended to six months if the particular employee's evaluation process feels incomplete. However, what exactly happens in this evaluation period?

There are two main things that I'm looking out for in every new member to our team: Attitude and Aptitude.

I look at how well they gel with my team, and whether or not they can at least carry their own weight. If there are any hints of a culture misfit, I will not allow this person to pass the evaluation period.

I also look at how well they get trained, and if they can perform their roles and responsibilities well. Therefore, KPIs are critical. KPIs and due dates should be regular and often—you shouldn't just have one right at the end of the evaluation period!

These KPIs must be agreed upon at the start of every evaluation period between the employee and their supervisor. If their KPIs are met, great.

If not, then there needs to be a follow-up plan answering the following questions:

- What are the areas that need improvement?
- What is the difference between the expected result and the actual result?
- How can things be improved?
- When should things be improved by?
- What resources are lacking in order for them to deliver the results, e.g. training, tutorials, mentorship, coaching, empowerment, etc.?

Unfortunately, not every hire will pass this stage. If you find that your new hire isn't aligned or cannot perform, then the best case might be to part ways. This is the case for current employees too, who may end up being unsuitable for your organisation for a variety of reasons. Whatever the case, when a team member has to leave, you'll need to go back to the recruitment stage to find the ideal candidate for the role.

The adage of "hiring slow, firing fast" is true, in this case. Be clear of the success criteria for your roles. Once you have that, ensure that your employees continually meet them. It is much better to have a role open than to have the wrong person in the role or in your company.

6. **Plan for progress**

   Every high-performer wants to know that there's a next step for them. Plan their career progression at your business and get their input and feedback about it. Examples of progression are to offer chances of exposure, progression, training and certification, and cross-disciplinary responsibilities.

   I look at regular training for my team, so that they can improve their skills and constantly learn new things. I also push them for things like events and awards where they can speak or represent the company, and for new roles that will challenge them.

   When you do this, it will create a hiring system which allows you to find, retain, and grow A-players in your organisation.

Chapter 17

WHAT TO DO WITH A-PLAYERS

I spent weeks and months trying to fill roles when I was running Vodien, so I know how difficult this process is. Sometimes there's a pressing need for talent, so every passing day feels like a wasted opportunity.

Once you do find someone and hire them, isn't it then time to break out the champagne and take a break?

Not so fast. Hiring someone is not the end of your duties as the boss. In fact, it's just the beginning. The onboarding process is something that's very critical to empowering your new employees, so make sure you don't neglect it.

It might feel like you deserve a break after all that work trying to recruit the person, but don't succumb to the temptation of just leaving your new hire alone while you go handle your other tasks (or drink that margarita that you've been hankering for, by the beach).

One of the greatest things that you can do in the onboarding stage is to communicate. And the number one thing that needs to be done is explaining a few things around your business. Most importantly, you need to explain the "Why" to your new employee. When you do this, it helps your new employees connect the "Why" to the "What" that they are doing.

The "Why" comes across in these five main areas that you'll need to explain to your new employees.

Explain Your Vision of the Company

Don't expect people to be mind readers. You need to tell your team why your company exists and what your vision is for the company.

This is especially important for new employees. Tell them what your company's vision is, your company's value proposition, and how your company is different from your competitors.

Explain the Relationship to External Stakeholders

Next, you'll need to connect the new employee in this grand vision of yours. Walk your employees through their job responsibilities and show them how their efforts matter to your customers.

The stronger a picture that you can paint, the greater the feeling of connection that your new employees will have.

This gives your employees a clear idea of why they're doing the tasks they're doing.

Explain the Relationship to Internal Stakeholders

A role in a company doesn't exist in a vacuum. There are other roles, oftentimes in other departments, that depend on that role.

This is clear to management and to the boss, but not as clear if you're an employee.

For example, it's hard for Engineering to think from Finance's point of view when Finance isn't approving new hardware purchases. It's much easier and much more common that people think everyone else is just trying to give them a hard time.

Explain Their Responsibilities

Don't assume that doing all of the above is sufficient. Your new employees need to know how exactly to do their roles.

This is where you need to explain your expectations, and check that they understand and agree to them.

Once that's done, you can have a system of checking in every few weeks to ensure that things are moving along smoothly. This is typically done with a monthly pulse or a monthly review.

This gives your new employees an avenue to feed back their thoughts about their work as well, and to raise any concerns that they might have.

Explain Why They Were Chosen

This is a great opportunity to show your new employees that they weren't just chosen out of desperation or luck. Tell them the exact reasons why they were ultimately chosen from the list of dozens of candidates.

If you have done your Job Description well, this point should be easy to pinpoint.

Every employee will appreciate this because you're praising them for attributes that they uniquely have. This reinforces why they're a great fit for the role and gives them validation to perform well at their role.

Transform New Employees into High Performers

Doing the five things above will set you apart from others, and most importantly, really empower your new employee hires. After all, you don't want just random individuals in your team. You want high performers who are effective and productive, and who are working together with you towards your company's vision.

Chapter 18

A POWERFUL COMPANY CULTURE

Company culture is important because it's an extension of the CEO, who might be the founder. If it is communicated well, your company culture gives your employees an idea of how to act and think that's best for the business.

A great company culture isn't about free beer and ping-pong tables. A great company culture incorporates the core values and vision that the founder has and has a supportive environment for people to do their best work.

Conversely, if the company culture is toxic, or if the CEO doesn't know how to communicate well, then the business will operate in chaos.

Employees are Only Looking for These Three Things

Contrary to popular belief, financial incentives are not going to create the performance that you want. If you think that you can simply create bonus schemes or salary increments and think that it will magically create team performance, then you are going to be gravely disappointed.

To create long-term performance requires much more in terms of motivation, and financial incentives are a terrible form of motivation.

Financial incentives form part of the minimum that employees want from your job but that will not motivate them to perform. Here are some more examples that will form minimums that people are looking for:

- Your office can't be a dump.
- You must have fair company policies.
- Your office equipment must be in good condition.

Besides a fair and equitable salary commensurate to the value that they bring to your business, there are only three things that high performers are looking for in their job: Meaning, Autonomy, and Mastery (Fig. 10).

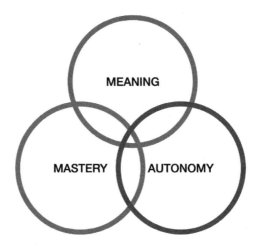

Fig. 10: The three elements high performers look for and how they overlap.

Meaning

Any high performer will tell you this: If there is no point in doing something, then why do it at all? High performers aren't interested in wasting their time, so everything that they do is highly purposeful.

In the same vein, if you expect A-players to be joining your team, then you can't expect them to be working on work that isn't impactful or meaningful.

This doesn't mean that everything needs to be innovative and groundbreaking. For something to have meaning, you just need to be clear on why it has meaning. There are two main ways entrepreneurs fail in this area. Work is meaningless when it is clearly "unoptimised", or when no meaning is ascribed to the work.

- **"Unoptimised" work**

  Sure, some amount of tedium is acceptable and sometimes necessary as well, but it can't form the majority of what they do. That's why we need the ARSAD funnel to ensure that work and processes are continually optimised for efficiency. (ARSAD will be covered in a later chapter.)

- **Work without meaning**

  Sometimes work may be important or meaningful, but the employee doesn't know or cannot see it. This is why communications is so important, which you will see in the **Cycle of Good Work** that I'll go through right after this section.

Autonomy

One of the differences between someone who is a high performer and someone who isn't is how much the person relishes autonomy.

What is autonomy? It's basically having the freedom to explore and complete a task. If you or a manager is constantly hounding and breathing down their necks, then there isn't autonomy.

In fact, doing that will only stifle creativity, innovation, and even mastery.

Mastery

Mastery is the ability to gain competence and ability in their skills and work. Everyone wants to feel like they are making progress and are getting better at what they do. Even better if they can get external validation of this, typically in the form of praise or recognition.

Fulfilling all these three components will result in high job satisfaction and subsequently, work performance.

However, to do this requires a lot of thought and planning in developing a solid company culture and work environment.

Cycle of Good Work

In Vodien, we used to operate on the Cycle of Good Work in order to develop a solid company culture, where we also provide what high performers are looking for.

The Cycle of Good Work consists of these five areas: Purpose, Ownership, Iteration, Education, Recognition (Fig. 11).

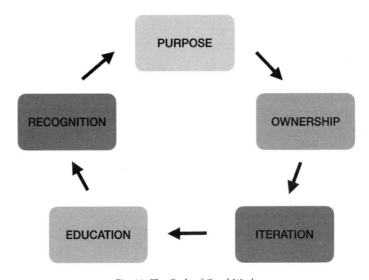

Fig. 11: The Cycle of Good Work.

These are five areas that directly address the three things that all employees look for in a job and company: Meaning, Autonomy, Mastery.

Once you have implemented these five areas in your business, you will find that you will have a very strong company core. That is what a strong company culture demands.

Purpose

Your role as leader of your business is to ensure that your team works on purposeful tasks.

None of your team should waste their time on processes that do not matter. If you allow your team to spend their time like that, you'll find that your employees will start to dread their work and question their tasks.

If it is work that matters, your role is to ensure that your team knows the significance and importance of what they're doing. You do this by clearly communicating your business vision and tying their tasks and results into the vision.

Sometimes, when new work is being introduced, such as new campaigns or new processes, then a lot of tedious, repetitive tasks are necessary. After all, everyone is still getting familiar with the new processes and figuring out what the tasks involve.

That's totally fine. What's not fine is if you let this continue and persist. "New work" should only be given a finite amount of time before it is systemised, and this is done through an iterative process of optimisation.

The worst case happens when you hear your employees start to complain, with statements like, "Oh, I don't know why I'm doing this work every day" or, "I'm spending so much time working on this, and nobody appreciates it".

Ownership

The next thing that must happen is that your team owns the tasks that they are working on. Accountability is a term that everyone tosses around, but true accountability cannot be had if there is no ownership of the task.

Have you seen children being told what to do versus doing something that they volunteered to do? As adults, we aren't much different. We all appreciate freedom and autonomy, and when we get it, it increases the sense of ownership that we have for the task.

It's difficult to get accountability for things that people don't have ownership of.

Iteration

People talk a lot about accepting failures. I think a better way to think about it is to have a mindset of iteration. That means accepting that mistakes are fine, because it's just another step in your path to success.

After all, Thomas Edison failed 10,000 times before he got to a working version of the lightbulb. When asked about it, he said, "I haven't failed. I've just found 10,000 ways that won't work."

That's typically how scientists work. And it's a process that entrepreneurs should also embrace. When faced with a new task i.e. wanting to get to a particular result (e.g. inventing a lightbulb), mistakes should be tolerated, meaning that experiments need to be performed.

The only caveat is having people on the team that make mistakes for no reason, or people who have no desire to make progress towards the business vision. Unfortunately, that is something that cannot be tolerated if the organisation is to become better and better over time.

Education

> *"When one teaches, two will learn."*
> *— Robert Heinlein*

Having a culture of teaching others is beneficial to everyone because:
- People get into the habit of documenting their processes, which makes it significantly easier to do process improvement on an organisational level.
- People get better at what they do and may even realise inefficiencies that can be improved upon in the process.
- People start training others in their roles so that the organisational capabilities rise as a whole. In addition, the individual can now go on vacations and not be disturbed or be promoted or rotated into another department/role because of the succession and redundancies that are developed.

This not only allows for people to do good work, it also sets up the organisation for success because it allows you to have a culture of documentation and having your team see work as processes.

Recognition

Finally, the last point in the Cycle of Good Work is recognition. Everyone appreciates praise or credit for the efforts that they put in.

People don't have to be given flowers or a celebration all the time. However, noting people's credit in projects or appreciating the hours or effort that they put in goes a long way.

This improves the self-worth of people, shows them that the sacrifices in the work they do is worthwhile, and gets them excited for the progress of the business vision.

Focusing on these five points will ensure that your team will get enjoyment and fulfilment working on meaningful tasks that tie in to the business vision.

Get More Super Scaling Resources

To help you with Super Scaling your business, I've created an online page just for you to access exclusive tools and resources. Scan the QR code on the left or go to:

SuperScaling.com/resources

Engage

EVOLVE
ENVISION
EMPOWER
ENGAGE
EXECUTE

"The key is when a customer walks away, thinking, 'Wow, I love doing business with them, and I want to tell others about the experience.' "
— *Shep Hyken*

ENGAGE is the next pillar of the 5E Scale Engine. We're talking about engagement with your customers and clients here. With any successful business, engagement is highly important.

Have you ever seen companies with great products that closed down? There are many reasons why these businesses don't succeed, but one reason could be poor customer engagement.

A lot of entrepreneurs suffer from the "build it, and they will come" syndrome. They are aiming to have their customers so happy that they can't wait to tell their friends all about their product. Unfortunately, it takes more than a great product to become a successful business.

You'll need to plan your customer journeys and ensure that you do the right things in the right sequence in order to engage your customers properly.

When you do engagement well, that's when it'll appear as though your product sells by itself.

Chapter 19

CUSTOMER JOURNEY

A customer isn't just the end user that consumes your product and pays you money. I think that definition is a little restrictive because it doesn't fully capture what a customer means to all kinds of businesses.

Instead, I define a customer as anyone whom your business serves. For example, if you are a marketplace, you have end-user consumers who are your customers, but you also have suppliers and merchants who are your customers.

Any Customer Journey for any organisation is made up of five key stages: Discovery, Consideration, Conversion, Fulfilment, Renewal (Fig. 12).

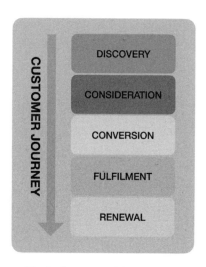

Fig. 12: The five key stages of the Customer Journey.

Most entrepreneurs spend their time at the Discover stage. The typical thought process is: "The more sales I get, the bigger I can grow my business". That's true for businesses in growth mode, but if your focus is now to get your businesses in scale mode, then it becomes absolutely false.

When you're scaling your business, the focus has to shift to a holistic improvement of the entire business, instead of just increasing sales. In fact, it's more important that you start focusing on the other stages of your Customer Journey, because it will cost you more than it will benefit you if you simply focus on sales alone.

Otherwise, it'll be akin to pouring more water into a leaky bucket. You can try to pour as much water in as you can, but because you are leaking water out, you'll never be able to ever retain as much water as someone with a non-leaky bucket of the same size.

To improve as a whole, you will need to ensure that all stages are performing optimally. You will need to focus on all activities and processes that can increase the key metrics of each stage.

In this new age of social media, negative reviews spread even more rapidly among people. Not only does a disgruntled customer's personal network gets influenced by their negative review, it spreads to thousands of friends, be it on Facebook, Instagram, LinkedIn, Twitter, or whatever new social network becomes popular. Even Google maintains a collection of reviews about your business that will either glorify you or vilify you in perpetuity.

That is why when people talk about your business in a positive way, you don't even need to spend that much on marketing anymore. The most powerful and reliable way to achieve this is to be utterly remarkable in everything you do for your customers. That means having products or services that are offering genuine value and an outstanding experience that's worth talking about.

How To Optimise Your Customer Journeys

When I looked at my Customer Journeys when I was running Vodien, it made me realise that there were three points that needed to be addressed at every stage:

- **Motivations**

  We need to be innately familiar with the motivations of our customers. What drives them to move on to the next stage of your Customer Journey?

- **Objections**

  Conversely, we need to also think about what objections your customers will have. What would turn them away? Are they still uncertain or uninformed? You should be proactively answering all the potential questions that your customers have so that they can progress through your Customer Journey smoothly.

- **Actions**

  These are the actions that are happening at each stage. To understand this, we just have to see what it is that the customer is doing at each stage. As a straightforward example, in the Conversion stage, your business has to collect payment. Typically, this means that the business needs to have payment processing facilities. Ideally, the more payment methods that are accepted, the better. Even better if financial payment plans are in place, especially with higher ticket items. This prevents a lot of friction that is involved when people consider their budgets and cash flow. To optimise this stage, you need to ask yourself what your business is currently doing at that stage. And more importantly, what your business should be doing in order to improve the results of that stage.

Let's look at each of the five stages in the Customer Journey model and examine how we can optimise them.

Discovery

In this stage, the customer is unaware of your business. The customer might even be unaware of your product or service, especially if what you have is more specialised.

Your job, at this stage, is to switch your customer from being unaware to being aware of your business and your product and services.

It is during the Discovery stage that you have all your marketing channels and campaigns. This typically spans Search Engine Optimisation (SEO), advertisements, and any other form of marketing.

Usually, the biggest problem that entrepreneurs face at this stage is not measuring their impact enough and not knowing which exact marketing channel to invest in.

This can all be optimised when you track everything, create proper processes, and have systems working for you.

Main Goals

- Attract customers to your business
- Educate customers

Sample Metrics

- Impressions
- Reach
- Search Engine Ranking
- Click-Through Rate (CTR)
- Quality Score

Consideration

After the customer is aware of your business and your products and services, you now need to prove that you will be a good choice.

The way to do this is typically through testimonials, ratings, reviews, samples, trials, and even presales with your company.

Proof, and especially social proof, is particularly powerful, even in the business-to-business or B2B space.

As client testimonials are to the B2C (business-to-consumer) space, case studies and client portfolios are to the B2B space. These pieces of proof go a long way to show that your business is in demand and is doing a good job at servicing your clients.

Other commonly used places of social proof are the search engines and social media platforms. Make sure you monitor these places for negative reviews, because you want to be showing that you respond proactively, professionally, and quickly.

Don't neglect presales channels as well. These include providing easy and multiple ways for customers to reach you for any presales questions, and also providing prompt and knowledgeable answers to their questions.

Your responsibility at this stage—and in all the other stages—is to do the best job you can at meeting your customers' needs. This is important because the customer is now aware at this point of time.

It can't be emphasised enough because at this stage, the customer can and will go to your competitor if you do a bad job at providing a good product or service.

This is all the more reason why you shouldn't spend money on increasing your sales if you do not have a business that is properly systemised.

If anything, you will have spent money educating and making these customers problem and solution-aware. However, because your business is "unoptimised", they will leave your business dissatisfied and go to your competitors instead.

Main Goals

* Convince customers that you are the best

Sample Metrics

* Search Engine Ranking
* Bounce Rate
* Engagement
* Time Spent On-Site
* Customer Satisfaction
* Wait Time
* Time to Resolution
* First Call Resolution

Conversion

At the Conversion stage, the customer turns into an actual customer from being a prospect.

This is easily measured as revenue, typically combined with optimising for average order value as well. You'd also measure conversion rate, which is your total leads/prospects over your total customers in a given period (e.g. a month).

To optimise this stage, you will need to work on having clear Call-to-Actions and an optimised checkout process that's well suited to your target audience.

In addition, you will also need to focus on things that can add value to your customers. The idea is not to spam your customers or rip them off, but to offer them value-added services and upgrades that they will appreciate and benefit from.

This covers everything from cross-selling and upselling, so make sure you think about everything that your customers might want from your product or service.

Remember the famous McDonald's example where cashiers always ask whenever they're taking an order: "Do you want fries with that?" Or "Would you like to upgrade that to a meal?"

These cross-sells and upsells are an easy way to give more to your customers, and easily add significant revenue.

Main Goals

- Convert customer
- Increase revenue per customer

Sample Metrics

- Conversion Rate
- Average Order Value
- Revenue
- Retargeting
- Cost-Per-Acquisition

Fulfilment

The next stage is Fulfilment, which I feel is an important part of the customer journey that most entrepreneurs typically do not give enough attention to.

As an entrepreneur, I feel that it is my responsibility to actually give my customers what they're looking for. As such, I structure my business accordingly, and the Fulfilment stage is so critical to me because this is where the customer is getting what they are paying for.

Like the other stages, the actions in this stage must be mapped out so that you know what is going on when a customer purchases from you.

Think about follow-ups, tutorials, guides, customer support, case studies, videos, and anything else that will promote and ensure customer success.

Customer success is crucial because you want your customers to be using your products and services. The more they use it, the more reliant they are on you, and the better it is for you as a business. The less they use it, the less reliant they are on you, and you are in serious danger of losing them as a customer (which affects the next stage, Renew).

The best way to ensure customer success is to get your customers to their goals. And customers all have goals. You just need to find out what they are.

Don't assume all customers are the same, and don't assume that all your customers have the same goals. Even something as seemingly straightforward as buying a meal from a restaurant business can stem from very different goals.

The customer's goal could simply be to be satiated, or perhaps he/she is looking to get proper nutrients, or maybe he/she wants to get a dining experience.

Each customer has his or her goals and it's your job to identify what they are. Don't assume that you know what the customer's goals are. Test! The closer you can get the customer to their goals, the better you'd do at customer success.

Main Goals	Sample Metrics
• Ensure customer success	• Customer Satisfaction
• Maintain high customer satisfaction	• Net Promoter Score (NPS)
• Promote positive advocacy	• Testimonials/Reviews

Renewal

Whenever I recommend a restaurant to my friends, and they do patronise it, I get very curious about whether they like the food or not. However, I've since learnt not to use the commonly asked question, "Do you like the food there?"

I don't know if you have realised this, but this question is terrible because you never get an honest answer back. It's not that people are liars or want to hide the truth—it's just that they are generally nice people. And when asked something like that, I find myself just giving a nice reply out of politeness too.

Therefore, I've learnt to change my question. I don't just ask if they liked the food; I ask if they would go back to the restaurant again. This frames the question a lot more concretely and gets them to really express their commitment level.

I believe that the best kind of vote is the one that requires commitment and action. Words are cheap, which is why surveys and polls might not necessarily be accurate.

You can get a lot more accurate by getting customers to actually part with their money. There's a difference between saying, "Yes, I'd buy this" and actually plonking down the money to pre-order or purchase something.

With your business, your greatest barometer of success is not your customer acquisition rate. Instead, it is your customer renewal rate.

The exact way this is manifested differs among businesses.

An SaaS (Software as a Service) business will look at the renewal of the customer's subscription, but not all businesses have subscriptions.

An F&B (Food and Beverage) business that's more traditional might look at a repeat purchase instead. It could be measuring whether or not the customer returns for another meal.

Similarly, for a service-based business like a consultancy firm or an agency, you're looking at customer renewals in the form of your customers taking on another contract or project with you.

That's why customer success in the Fulfil stage is so important. You absolutely need to get your customers to fall in love with your products and services. And the more that they use and rely on your products and services, the better.

On top of customer success, you need a system that alerts you to customer failure too. That's what happens when a customer starts showing signs that they're going to leave you.

Ideally, your customer success programmes are so perfect that you don't ever need to consider about customer failure, but sometimes customers slip through the cracks. We need to have systems in place to handle these cases as well, so that you can right what went wrong and salvage the relationship.

When I had my customers, I would be happy if I saw customers having continued use of their services. If a customer's account suddenly went dark and had no activity, then I'd be very alarmed. This either means that the customer isn't getting value from my service or has already found an alternative service.

What are some other examples? Well, if you are a subscription-based service and they haven't logged into your system for a really long time, that's a red flag. Or if they have no usage recently. Or worse, if they are visiting pages in your FAQ talking about cancellation or refunds.

Any of these activities should immediately raise red flags. These should kick someone in your team to immediately reach out to them, find out what's wrong, and try to salvage the relationship.

Main Goals

- Ensure renewal
- Promote positive advocacy
- Reduce churn

Sample Metrics

- Churn Rate
- Referrals
- Testimonials/Reviews

Chapter 20

SCALABLE MARKETING CHANNELS

In your business, you will have to build multiple marketing channels. Depending on your business, these will differ.

No one will know what works for your business. The best way to approach this is using a scientific approach, where you systematically experiment with various marketing channels, while being meticulous about your variables, just like a scientific experiment. Ensure that you tightly control your expenditure, time, and closely monitor the results.

After all, the only way to know what works is to dip your toes into the water to test the water's temperature, rather than to dive right in. This means testing unexplored marketing channels first, before investing 100% in them.

For some businesses, Facebook ads may be more effective. Other businesses might benefit from Instagram instead. Some businesses could even do really well with Google's Display Network, or even sponsorships in targeted publications.

Whatever the channel is, and whatever your assumptions or pre-conceived notions are, make sure you test everything. The key is to do it like how scientists would—in the form of controlled experiments.

I've found that you can never take someone else's experience as gospel truth. Their experience with marketing channels can act as a guideline for you, but never replace you actually testing it out for your own business.

Finding the right marketing channels can produce big results for your business, resulting in a surge of leads and revenue. And if you're an early adopter of an effective channel, it can give you a serious head start on your competition.

Initial users of Google Adwords and Facebook advertising were able to generate big results at a relatively low cost before those channels became saturated.

But how do you find these highly productive marketing channels?

With so many options available, it can feel like an overwhelming task. Should you focus on Search Engine Optimisation (SEO) or Pay-Per-Click (PPC)? Podcasting or videos? Social media or blogging? How can you know where to invest your time and money?

In this section, we're going to walk you through the process of finding, testing, and growing your marketing channels.

Ready? Let's get started.

Controlled Experimentation

The first step in finding effective marketing channels is testing and experimenting. You simply won't know if a marketing channel will work for your business unless you test it. You have to constantly experiment, testing a variety of channels until you find the ones that really drive significant results.

How can you find these different marketing channels? There are several ways:

- **Analyse your competition**

    Digital marketing tools like Ahrefs and SEMRush can give you a sense of what your competitors are doing with SEO, content marketing, and PPC. The Facebook Ad Library can give you insight into the types of social media ads they're running. Look at the most successful businesses in your space and determine what marketing channels they're using. Can you make those same channels work for you?

- **Analyse your audience**

    In many ways, your audience will dictate which marketing channels you choose. You want to focus on the channels your audience uses. If your audience is young, you may want to consider a platform like Instagram, since it tends to be favoured by millennials and younger. If your audience is older, you may have more success using Facebook or even direct mail. If you target business professionals, your best choice may be LinkedIn or email marketing.

- **Analyse your own business**

  Some marketing channels may be a better fit for your business than others. If you run a service-based business, you may want to focus on local SEO so that you connect with customers in your area. If you're an SaaS (Software as a Service) company, you may get the most benefit from social media advertising.

- **Analyse current trends**

  Websites like Hubspot, TechCrunch, and AdAge can help you be aware of current marketing trends and potentially untapped marketing channels.

The bottom line is that you won't know if a channel works until you actually test it. Identify the channels that you think will be the most profitable and then begin testing and experimenting.

Give Sufficient Time and Effort

When testing a channel, only evaluate the results after you've given enough time and resources to it. This will look different depending on the channel. SEO requires a fair amount of time and effort before you will start seeing significant results. With PPC, on the other hand, you can generate results much more quickly.

Be realistic as you contemplate which channels to use. Don't start using a channel unless you're willing to use it for a sufficient length of time and invest the appropriate amount of effort.

Also, don't give up on or dive into a marketing channel until you've done a sufficient number of experiments. If you're doing PPC, create numerous variations of and target audiences for your ads. If you're doing email marketing,

A/B test various subject lines, calls-to-action, and formats. If you're focusing on video, test different lengths, titles, meta descriptions, etc.

If you don't thoroughly experiment with a channel, you may end up abandoning it prematurely.

Focus Your Efforts

You may be tempted to jump into five different marketing channels at once, but don't do it. There are several reasons for this.

First, you'll end up getting spread far too thin. You'll end up only being able to spend a small amount of time on each channel, limiting the value each channel provides. As a result, your marketing campaigns will be mediocre at best.

Imagine trying to simultaneously create PPC ads, emails, blog posts, podcasts, and webinars. Unless you have a large team at your disposal, the quality will be very low or you simply won't get everything done. You also won't be able to effectively engage with your audience, which is especially important with most forms of digital marketing.

On the other hand, when you focus on a single channel, you can master it. You learn the ins and outs of it, and you discover which strategies are most effective. The more you master a channel, the higher your ROI (return on investment) and the lower the cost of using that channel becomes.

Second, trying to manage a bunch of new channels at once is chaotic. You'll feel overwhelmed as you try to create content, analyse the results, and optimise your efforts. You'll miss key details and will probably fall behind on things. You'll get burnt out and will be tempted to throw in the towel.

Focusing on a single channel allows you to give it all your attention. You can ensure that everything is working as it should be and that nothing is slipping through the cracks.

Finally, focusing on one channel at a time is much more cost effective. If you pour money into a bunch of channels at once, your ROI will be significantly lower and you'll blow through your budget much faster. When you focus your efforts, you can get the maximum results from your budget.

Double Down on What Works

Your results will probably vary wildly depending on the marketing channel you choose. Some of your experiments will be spectacular successes. Others will be abject failures. Still others will produce only mediocre results. That's why they're called "experiments".

In order to know which channels are most effective, you need to closely track your results. If you can't determine the ROI of a particular marketing channel, you have no way of knowing whether it's really working for you. You need to know how much it costs you to acquire a new lead and then convert that lead into a paying customer. You need to have a clear understanding of how leads flow into your marketing funnel and translate into revenue.

Additionally, you need to know your Customer Lifetime Value (LTV). Knowing your LTV allows you to determine exactly how much you want to spend on customer acquisition. For example, say you sell a product for $10. If you only focus on the initial sale, you won't want to spend more than $10 to acquire a new customer. However, if you know that your LTV is $100, you can afford to spend much more on customer acquisition.

Obviously, if a channel is a spectacular success, you should double down on it. Invest more time and money into the channel while still closely tracking your results.

If it's a spectacular failure, then you probably shouldn't keep investing in it. Focus on other, more profitable channels.

If the channel produces mediocre results, then you have a decision to make. You can try to continue to optimise the channel in hopes of getting better results or you can focus your efforts elsewhere.

Optimise Your Campaigns

Once you've identified an effective marketing channel, you need to optimise your marketing campaigns. In other words, you need to keep testing and tweaking your efforts so that you continue getting maximum value from the channel.

If you don't keep optimising, your campaigns will grow stagnant over time. People will stop responding to your marketing efforts. Keywords will become unprofitable. Specific headlines and images will stop being interesting to customers. Competitors will move in, saturating the channel, and making it harder to stand out.

The bottom line is that you can't put your marketing on autopilot. You have to continually be looking for strategic ways to improve your marketing and separate yourself from your competitors. You need to think outside the box and not simply do what everyone else is doing. Just because something has worked well in the past doesn't mean that it will continue to work well in the future.

Do the Work

Identifying effective marketing channels takes a significant amount of time and effort. Running multiple experiments isn't necessarily easy. Constantly tracking and analysing your results requires commitment. Consistently optimising your campaigns so they don't stagnate is no small task.

But the work is worth it. When you find the right marketing channels and create highly effective campaigns within those channels, you get outsized results. You can drive growth in your company like never before. If you look at the most successful companies, they all have a commitment to finding highly effective marketing channels and then leveraging those channels for all they're worth.

So do the work. Run the experiments. Double down on what works and cut out what doesn't. Optimise until you're getting maximum value from a channel. And repeat.

You won't regret it.

Chapter 21

THE NEW-AGE SALES APPROACH

At its largest, Vodien had a staff count of 150. Of the 150, we had five people in sales, and over a hundred in customer support. That should give you an idea of the value that we placed in customer retention and fulfilment of our service.

After speaking to several people, I've realised that some people view this in a different manner. They view the sales function as a profit centre, and the customer support function as a cost centre (Fig. 13).

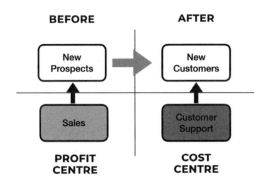

Fig. 13: For some, Sales is a profit centre while Customer Support is a cost centre, thus the reluctance to focus more on the latter.

Your business needs customers to thrive. No revelation there. When you look at businesses, there are only three ways that you can get more revenue:

• Getting more customers;

- Getting more customers to pay you more; and/or
- Getting more customers to pay you more often.

When it comes to growing your business, you have to walk a fine line between acquiring new customers while also keeping your existing ones. After all, it doesn't help your business if you get new customers and lose current customers at the same rate.

Most businesses make the grave mistake of chasing after new customers instead of nurturing existing ones. Instead, a holistic manner of acquiring new customers and also retaining existing ones will ensure that you have a solid way of growing your business (Fig. 14).

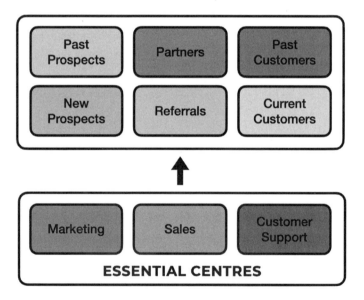

Fig. 14: A holistic approach is to view Marketing, Sales, and Customer Support as essential centres that will garner new customers as well as retain existing ones, thus growing your business.

So how do you walk this line effectively without losing your way? That's what we're going to explore in this section. We're going to:

- Explain the difference between customer acquisition and retention, along with important metrics you need to evaluate;

- Explain why customer retention is so important and deserves your focus; and
- Give you concrete strategies for improving your customer retention.

Ready? Let's get started.

Customer Acquisition and Retention

First, let's make sure we're clear on exactly what we mean by acquisition and retention.

Customer acquisition is simply the process of acquiring new customers. It includes everything from initially attracting potential customers to finally convincing them to purchase from you. Your marketing funnel is designed to help you acquire customers.

Customer retention is keeping the customers you've already acquired. It involves getting customers to stay with you over time and make repeated purchases.

Customer Acquisition Cost (CAC) is the amount you have to spend to obtain one customer. It's calculated by totalling all the sales and marketing costs in a given period and then dividing that by the number of customers gained.

For example, if you spend $1,000 in sales and marketing and you acquire ten customers, your CAC is $100. The better your customer retention rate, the more you can afford to spend on acquiring new customers since those customers will spend more money.

Churn rate is the percentage of customers that you lost during a given time. If you had 100 customers at the beginning of the month and 90 at the end of the month, your churn rate is 10%. The more you can reduce your churn rate, the higher your customer retention rate will be.

Customer Lifetime Value (LTV) is the average total amount customers spend with you over the course of your relationship with them. It's very important to calculate the LTV for your different customer segments. Why? Because each segment that has different pricing models will result in different LTVs.

For example, say you sell cars and you have a $30,000 model and a $70,000 model. The customer types for each model will be very different. Even with the higher prices, the $70,000 segment may not have a higher LTV than the first.

When you know your LTV numbers, you know how much you can spend on acquiring new customers. You will also know if your efforts on developing strong customer relationships and improving customer success has resulted in improvements, because if they have, you will see your LTV increase.

There are many formulae to calculate your LTV and you can find all of them with a quick Google search. For a simple explanation, we will use a simple LTV calculation. We will just need to know how long your customer's average lifetime is with you (in terms of months), and how much your average monthly profit is per customer.

When we multiply these two figures together, we will get your estimated LTV number.

Acquisition or Retention: Which Matters More?

So which matters more, customer acquisition or retention? Obviously, both are important. If your business doesn't acquire customers, you won't grow. You need to get new customers in order to cover your costs and make money.

The problem, however, is that many business owners focus a huge portion of their attention and budget on acquisition and don't give nearly as much thought to retention. They spend a huge amount of time and money on attracting and converting new customers and neglecting their existing customers. This is problematic for a number of reasons.

First, getting new customers is much more expensive than retaining existing ones. While it varies by industry, it's estimated that it costs somewhere between five to twenty-five times (Gallo) more to acquire new customers than hold on to current ones.

This means that if it costs $500 to get a new customer, it will cost you $100 or less to keep current customers.

Second, increasing retention has a big impact on profits, with a 5% increase translating into a 25–95% jump in profits (Reichheld). Third, existing customers convert at a much higher rate of 60–70% as compared to acquiring new ones, which is typically around 5–20% (Hull).

Fourth, the cost of getting new customers to the same revenue levels as loyal customers is sixteen times higher. What's more, existing customers spend up to 31% more than new customers (Saleh).

Starting to get the picture? Customer retention is hugely important. Acquiring new customers is so much more expensive than retaining existing ones, and retention has a much higher ROI.

If you need further proof of this, look at how much effort and money Amazon spends getting people into their Prime programme. They offer free shipping, streaming video and music, exclusive deals, and much more. Why do they go to so much effort? Because they know that once a person is part of Prime, they'll spend a lot more money with Amazon.

As Pamela Danziger writes in Forbes:

> *"An astounding 85% of Prime shoppers visit Amazon at least once a week, while 56% non-Prime shoppers report the same. ... Further, over 45% of Prime members purchase on Amazon at least once a week. Its success rate with non-members is far behind, with only 13% reporting weekly purchases."*

Amazon knows the value of customer retention and they're willing to invest large amounts of money to keep customers coming back again and again.

Of course, all this raises a key question: how can you improve your customer retention?

8 Strategies for Improving Customer Retention

Now that you know the importance of focusing on retaining existing customers, let's talk about specific strategies for doing that.

1. **Create a superior customer experience**

    Developing loyal customers starts with creating a superior customer experience. It doesn't matter how great your product or service is if customers don't like purchasing from you. If they don't have a good experience, they'll take their business somewhere else.

    Some of the most successful brands have been built on the backs of incredible customer service. Warby Parker doesn't sell the cheapest or highest quality glasses. What they do offer is outstanding customer service. When you call the company, a real person answers the phone within seconds. You don't have to navigate complex phone menus or talk to a robot who will inevitably misunderstand what you want. While this may seem like a small thing, it creates a real connection between the brand and their customers.

    The stories about Trader Joe's customer service have become legendary. Though the grocery store doesn't normally deliver, one employee delivered groceries to an elderly man in the midst of a snowstorm so that he would have enough food and not have to venture out into inclement weather (Ciotti).

    In the same vein, Zappos—an online shoe and clothing retailer—is known for an obsessive focus on creating outstanding customer experiences. In 2012, one customer service rep chatted with a customer for a whopping ten hours (Fabbioni)!

    If you want to retain customers, think strategically about how you can delight your customers. It isn't especially complicated. Make it simple for customers to contact you via a variety of channels and work hard to address all problems that arise. Engage with customers on social media and give employees the freedom to do whatever is necessary to serve customers. Try to go above and beyond the norm to give your customers an experience they won't forget.

When you focus on giving customers a great experience, they'll keep coming back again and again. What's more, they'll spread the word about your company, which can result in increased customer acquisition.

As Sarah Chambers, founder of Supported Content and a Customer Support Consultant, notes:

> *"When it comes to standing out against entrenched competitors, it's critical for businesses to find their moments of opportunity. It's rarely practical to compete on price or efficiency. However, new and growing stores do have a set of differentiators worth investing in: product, brand, and customer service.*
>
> *Companies that focus on creating meaningful customer experiences can choose to compete on loyalty and word-of-mouth, beat the behemoths, and carve out their own place in the market."*

2. Focus on solving customer problems

When building a business, it's easy to get caught up in the details about the product or service you're offering. You can get so focused on adding this feature or that option to the point that you forget about your customers.

Ultimately, your success depends on how well you can solve the problems of your customers. The better you are at solving problems and meeting desires, the more your customers will want to shop with you.

Jeff Bezos has turned Amazon into a world-altering company by focusing on solving problems for his customers. In his own words (Haden):

> *"[I]n our retail business, we know that customers want low prices, and I know that's going to be true ten years from now. They want fast delivery; they want vast selection.*
>
> *It's impossible to imagine a future ten years from now where a customer comes up and says, 'Jeff, I love Amazon; I just wish the prices were a little higher.' 'I love Amazon; I just wish you'd deliver a little more slowly.' Impossible.*
>
> *And so the effort we put into those things, spinning those things up, we know the energy we put into it today will still be paying off dividends for our customers ten years from now. When you have something that you know is true, even over the long term, you can afford to put a lot of energy into it."*

Bezos knows that when it comes to online shopping, people want it to be easy, quick, and low-priced. And so he has focused relentlessly on eliminating friction from the shopping experience and lowering prices.

When it comes to your business, what customer problems are you ultimately trying to solve? How can you do that more effectively? Do any of your activities not contribute to solving the problems better? If so, it may be time to re-evaluate whether you should be doing those things.

Don't get the shiny object syndrome. What can you offer that no one else does? Shopify originally started out selling snowboarding equipment. Eventually, they realised that they were better at creating online shopping stores and set out to make it easy for anyone to create a store. Now they're a billion-dollar company.

3. **Set appropriate expectations**

When initially engaging with new customers, it's essential that you set appropriate expectations. You need to understand what they want and then set expectations regarding how you'll meet those desires.

For example, say you're an Search Engine Optimisation (SEO) agency. Your clients want to rank higher in Google searches and they want to do that as quickly as possible. You need to help them understand both how long the process typically takes and what sorts of results they can expect.

Don't make promises you can't fulfil. Set reasonable expectations and then work hard to exceed those expectations. If you do exceed them, your customers will love you for it. But whatever you do, don't do less than expected.

If, for some reason, you fail to meet expectations, honestly apologise to the customer, explain what had happened, and offer to compensate them in some way. Most people are reasonable and understand that things happen.

4. **Create an effective onboarding programme**

When a new customer purchases your product or service, they may need help in understanding how to use it effectively. If they can't quickly figure out how to use it, they'll become frustrated and not use it at all. The more you can simplify and speed up the education process, the more likely it is that customers will want to keep working with you.

There are a number of different ways you can effectively onboard new customers. You can have a customer service rep work directly with new customers and tailor the training specifically to their business. You can create an automated email sequence that goes out to new customers, guiding them through different actions they can take. You can create a robust resource library where customers can find the answers to all their questions.

The better your onboarding process, the lower your churn rate will be. Customers will understand how to use your product or service and will have significantly more success.

5. **Consistently get customer feedback**

   You can't improve your customer retention process if you don't know what your customers are thinking. You need a process for getting feedback from them, consistently review it, and then take appropriate action.

   There are a number of really simple ways to get feedback from customers. Many businesses use the Net Promoter Score, where customers are asked how likely they are to recommend the business to a friend. You can also utilise user testing, focus groups, customer surveys, etc.

   Once you've gathered feedback, examine it and look for common patterns. Are there any complaints that tend to come up repeatedly? Are there any specific features that customers really like or dislike? Identify the common trends, and then take action to improve the overall customer experience.

6. **Regularly communicate with customers**

   For any relationship to thrive, regular communication is essential. The same goes for your relationship with your customers. They need to regularly hear from you so that you're never far from their minds. Regular communication nurtures your relationship with them and keeps them coming back repeatedly.

   Start by developing a communication calendar where you map out how often you'll communicate and by what method. Determine whether you'll call them, send emails, text messages, physical mail, or some combination of these. Also, map out the content that you'll include in your communications, whether that be tips for using your product, discount codes, news, etc.

   Once you've mapped out your content calendar, seek to automate the process as much as possible. For example, create a post-sale email sequence that automatically gets sent to new customers after they purchase from you. Automating the process ensures that things don't slip through the cracks and that you stay in regular communication with customers. If you don't automate the process, it will be difficult for you to stay on top of everything.

7. **Develop a loyalty programme**

Loyalty programmes are a time-tested method for getting customers to keep coming back. They benefit both you and your customers. You get the benefit of repeat business and they get special rewards that less loyal customers don't get.

It makes sense from a revenue perspective as well. Studies have shown that customers who connect to your brand emotionally have a lifetime value more than three times greater than average customers. This feeling of being connected to the brand also results in the customer spending twice as much as customers who rate themselves as just satisfied with the brand (Motista).

As Sophia Bernazzani, who started and managed the HubSpot Service Blog, notes:

"In this day and age, customers are making purchase decisions based on more than just the best price— they're making buying decisions based on shared values, engagement, and the emotional connection they share with a brand. Customer loyalty programmes are a great way to engage with customers beyond just the point of purchase, to interface on shared values, and to provide even more value to customers—making them happier and more likely to keep purchasing from you."

8. **Focus on fostering authentic relationships**

A key way to stand out from the competition while also improving customer retention is to focus on fostering authentic relationships with customers. We live in an increasingly digital world, with so much interaction happening online. When your customers see that there are real people behind your company, it fosters a connection between you and them. They realise that you're not just a company that cares about the bottom line.

How can you develop meaningful relationships with customers? Some simple ways include:

- Regularly interact with them on social media, answering questions, responding to comments, etc.;
- Include photos of real employees on your website so that visitors get a sense of who makes up the company;
- Add personal touches wherever possible, such as handwritten notes, personalised emails, phone calls, etc.

Your goal is simply to make your customers feel like they actually matter to you. When you do that, they're much more likely to stick around for the long haul.

Customers are Your Greatest Assets

Your customers are your greatest asset, and you should treat them as such. Yes, they provide much needed revenue. They also can act as your most powerful marketing tactic. When you work hard to keep your customers, you end up providing them with an excellent experience.

In turn, they tell their friends and family about it and may even talk about it on social media. This strengthens your brand in the eyes of potential customers and can drive customer acquisition.

Few things are more powerful than word-of-mouth marketing. Nielson reports that 92% of people give more weight to recommendations from friends and family than any other type of advertising.

All this is to say, working hard on customer retention is worth the effort. While it may not be nearly as sexy as acquisition, it's absolutely critical for your business. It leads to more revenue, a higher LTV, a lower churn rate, and a stronger bottom line.

Perhaps most importantly, it helps you build a company that actually makes a difference. People actually care about your business. For decades, retail company L.L. Bean had an unlimited returns policy. No matter the reason or age of the product, you could return it if you didn't like it.

The result? L.L. Bean has a massively loyal customer base who are committed to purchasing from the company.

So do the hard work of customer retention. Focus on creating amazing customer experiences and solving people's thorniest problems. Set reasonable expectations and then seek to exceed them. Work hard to onboard new customers and then regularly listen to their feedback. Regularly communicate with customers, reward your most loyal ones, and strive to foster authentic relationships with them.

If you do these things, you'll create an army of fans who will come back to your company again and again.

Get More Super Scaling Resources

To help you with Super Scaling your business, I've created an online page just for you to access exclusive tools and resources. Scan the QR code on the left or go to:

SuperScaling.com/resources

Execute

"Time is what we want most, but what we use worst."
— William Penn

Only after you've worked on all four pillars can you move on to the final pillar, which is EXECUTE.

The most limited resource on our hands is time. However, most of us live as though it's our most abundant. I think one of the reasons why we do this is because humans have a natural inability to perceive very large numbers. Time, even though finite, can be large in quantity.

Think about one billion. That's a really big number. If you had a billion dollars, and assuming you had a fairly generous salary of $250,000 a year, and zero interest or returns on the balance amount, you would take four thousand years to spend it all.

Here's another number that's a bit smaller than a billion—42 million. Can you imagine what to do with 42 million minutes? You'd probably feel paralysed at the sheer number of minutes, or absolutely disinterested because it's too big to grasp properly. Well, the average human life span is eighty years. That's 42,048,000 minutes. Turns out 42 million minutes is the average human life span.

When we look at the entirety of 42 million minutes, the typical response is to freeze and not know how to begin comprehending it. However, time will still pass by. The key to live an effective life isn't to plan everything out at once. We don't ask ourselves "How do I live eighty years effectively?"

Instead, our lives are made up of smaller projects and chapters that might span several years at a time.

When you think about time in large, abstract numbers, it's difficult to construct effective strategies to use it effectively. That's one of the reasons why inefficiencies start to creep into our lives. We have to design tools and models to help us manage time, which is how we're going to approach increasing efficiency in our businesses.

One of the things that I hate is inefficiency. That's why I've been absolutely ruthless in my businesses to optimise, delegate, eliminate, and automate processes whenever I can.

Focusing on increasing efficiency increases your business's throughput and productivity, reduces resource wastage, and allows you to scale up because you now no longer have the constraints that you used to have.

It's like a sprinter who weighs 30 kg extra—it's going to be hard winning races with that extra weight. However, with the right tools, you can lose that weight and start being competitive. Similarly, I can give you the tools and know-how so that your business can shed any extra fat. Immediately, you'll be unencumbered and be able to train and perform at your optimal levels.

Now as a business, you need this performance from your entire organisation—which includes everyone, not just your star people. That means you have to consider how to increase efficiency across the board.

As you can imagine, this changes you from an entrepreneur with a group of employees to someone who's leading a proper organisation. This transforms your business from something you work in into something you work on. Your business becomes a well-oiled machine, allowing you to focus on strategy and growth.

The key factors that contribute to having more efficiency and higher performance in your company's projects are to:

- Simplify your process and projects;
- Decrease specificity of subject matters;
- Decrease dependency on "bottlenecked" resources;
- Increase transparency and documentation; and
- Increase training.

Some of these things are harder to work on than the others. For example, some processes and projects are inherently complex—simplifying them might not be possible.

Specificity is also tied to certain tasks. If the role requires copywriting knowledge, you're not going to be able to hire anyone off the street and have them produce great copy overnight.

However, the rest can definitely be worked on. For instance, transparency and documentation is absolutely necessary for a business to perform better and can be implemented in any business.

With documentation, the end goal is for everyone in the team to know what everyone else is working on. Any working files are openly accessible to everyone with the right access levels. In addition, anyone in the team can understand how work is performed because processes are documented clearly.

To systematically increase efficiency, we use a framework called the ARSAD Funnel, which I'll cover next.

Chapter 22

DESIGN A PROCESS THE RIGHT WAY

"If you can't describe what you are doing as a process, you don't know what you're doing."
— W. Edwards Deming

A business is essentially a group of people that work on tasks. We need to know who does what, and when, so that we can improve the production time and quality of the results.

All tasks that a business works on has two essential components: People and Processes.

Thinking of tasks in terms of processes creates consistency in the form of a clear road map for anyone in your team to follow, to get from A to B.

The clearer we are at defining processes, the better we get at time savings, cost control, and quality. Clearly defined processes ensure that people don't have to remember how to determine how to do the task every single time. This greatly reduces the risk of human error and increases quality.

Process Simplification Questions

These questions can help structure our simplification efforts and get us working on the right things.

Feedback
- What feedback do you get from people using the process?
- What feedback do you get from people receiving the output from the process?

Metrics
- What are the existing metrics for this process?
- What will the new metrics be for the simplified process?

Process Map
- Which steps add value and which do not?
- Are there any steps that cause a rework?
- Is the process easily accessible?
- Is the process easily understandable?
- Is the documentation easily understandable?
- Are roles and responsibilities clear and relevant?

Innovation
- How can this process be completely redesigned?
- How can a new tool or technology improve this process?
- How can steps be automated?

Optimisation
- How can waiting time be reduced between steps?
- Can any steps be combined?
- Can any steps run in parallel?
- Can any steps be standardised?
- Can any cycle times be reduced?

- Are all approval steps necessary?
- What other dependent processes cause roadblocks for this process?

Quality

- Which steps are there to ensure quality?
- What is the consequence of making a mistake at these steps?
- Is there someone checking the work, and is that step necessary?

Consistency

- Is the output (i.e. documents, code, etc.) consistent across all processes? If not, how do we make it consistent so that maintenance costs are lowered?
- Are the tools/systems standardised across all processes? If not, how do we make it consistent so that maintenance costs are lowered?

Communications

- How resilient is the flow of communication?
- Are there potential bottlenecks if the method of communication fails (e.g. email server or service outages) or a person leaves (e.g. stored emails lost)?

Documents

- Which documents are necessary and which can be removed (duplicates or waste)?
- Are hard copies necessary? Where are they stored? Why are they stored?
- Are multiple copies necessary? How can duplication be removed?
- Is all content in a document necessary?
- Which forms can be removed?
- How can the forms be processed and stored better?

Regulatory Requirements

- What steps are absolutely necessary for fulfilling regulatory requirements, and what can be removed without much disruption to the results?

Stakeholders

- Would all stakeholders be happy with the simplified process?
- Will the decision-maker approve the simplified process?

How to Create Processes

A simple process can really be documented in any medium. It can even be created with pen and paper, though I think there are much more efficient methods.

Personally, I prefer creating more complex processes in a flow chart software. There are many free versions online that you can use for this.

A basic process has the following format. Each symbol is for a specific function when drawing flow charts (Google is your friend), but this isn't a book about flow charts so I won't go into detail about it.

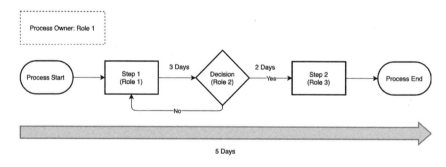

Fig. 15: A flow chart to map out a simple process.

With diagrams like Fig. 15, you and your team will be able to visually understand the flow of processes in your organisation.

The important points are:

- Amount of time taken between steps;
- The owners of each step, especially with regards to decision making.

Fig. 16 is an example of a process in a company that describes an ad creation process. It answers the following points:

What: What happens when we need to create an ad creative?

When: When a Project Manager initiates the process

Who: Project Manager and Designer

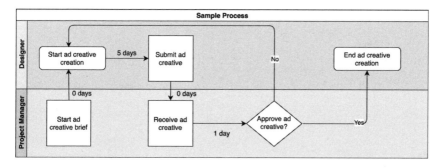

Fig. 16: A sample flow chart showing the ad creation process in a company.

Once a task has been clearly defined with its people and processes, the task can now go through the ARSAD Funnel that we will discuss in the next chapter.

Chapter 23

SYSTEMATICALLY INCREASING BUSINESS EFFICIENCY

One of the grails of entrepreneurs and business owners is to increase business efficiency. After all, time is our scarcest resource.

If you're trying to scale your business right now, you must know the feeling of being strangled for time.

That's how I felt when I was scaling Vodien. Everything in your business is demanding time from you and as a result, time becomes such a scarce resource.

I felt so frustrated at the shortage of time that I started looking at how best to manage time, free time up, maximise productivity, and increase business efficiency.

I wanted to squeeze every single amount of productivity out from the time that I was spending on my business. However, it's easier said than done. Increasing productivity is difficult to do on a personal basis, and exponentially more difficult to do on an organisational level. There are so many moving parts in a business and things change all the time.

If you and your team members are doing things on an ad hoc basis and reactively most of the time, I can assure you that you'll soon get overwhelmed, because that was exactly what happened to me initially.

The only way to improve things is by having a systematic approach when you're thinking about how to increase business efficiency. This allows for sustainable and scalable growth.

Why Systems Are So Powerful

If you have the mindset of being systematic in order to increase business efficiency, you start developing structured and sustainable ways to make permanent improvements in your business.

This was one of the more important concepts that allowed me to transform and scale up Vodien successfully.

I call the methodology that I use to create this hyper-focus to increase business efficiency, the ARSAD Funnel.

Increasing Efficiency with the ARSAD Funnel

The ARSAD Funnel has these five steps: Analyse, Remove, Simplify, Automate, Delegate (Fig. 17).

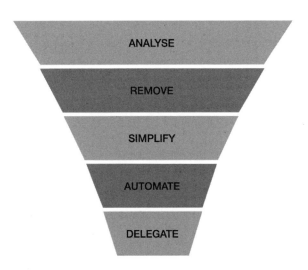

Fig. 17: The five steps of the ARSAD Funnel.

Analyse

The first thing that you need to do is to take a step back and analyse the work that is being done in your business.

A good way is to do this is with every person in your organisation, individually.

Everyone will have to log all the tasks that they're doing so that the type of tasks and the time used for each task is clear. With this, you can spot the inefficiencies and the areas of improvement.

The easiest areas to increase business efficiency can be found in recurring tasks and the tasks that take up too much time.

It's crucial to understand where time is being spent, and then you can move on to answering the following questions:

- What are the assumptions that you have with regards to the tasks, why they exist, and their utility?
- What is the purpose of every task, and is this purpose being met?
- What tasks are being done regularly?
- How long does each task take to completion?

Remove

Next, you need to look at removing any process that's unnecessary or low impact. This is essentially trimming the fat from the operations in your business.

I find this an absolutely crucial first step to take, and I don't see enough people following this sequence of action. Too many people look at automation or simplification or delegation first, which ends up overly complicating matters.

The importance of the sequence reminds me of road bicycle racing enthusiasts. In road cycling, the weight that the cyclists carry affects their cycling speeds.

Some road cyclists try to improve their cycling times by investing in really expensive gear, such as carbon fibre parts in order to reduce the weight of their bicycles. These parts are typically very expensive but can result in 50–500% savings in weight. However, because bicycles aren't very heavy to begin with, these percentages translate into absolute amounts of a few hundred grams.

It boggles my mind, because these same cyclists aren't the leanest that they can be. If they lose some body fat, they can get much more weight savings. This not only makes the weight on the bike lower—it's cheaper than buying expensive gear—but also much better for your health and fitness.

It's the same thing as scaling up businesses and trying to increase business efficiency. Losing body fat is painful and not as fun as buying new gear. However, the ones who truly are committed and dedicated to improving themselves will do it.

I can guarantee that not everything is necessary in your business operations. You might find that you might even be able to close down entire product lines and come out leaner and faster and more profitable as a result.

Here's a simple example. One of the things that we removed was the payment method of cash. Cash was something that we thought was a requirement to deal with traditional businesses.

However, cash, as a payment method, was a hassle. We needed someone to attend to the clients who came down physically to hand over the cash payment. We had to count the cash accurately and provide accurate change. We had to hold an amount of cash in the office as a result also, and spend time depositing the cash at the bank.

Besides the time that was required for this whole process, there was also huge risks of human error in counting the wrong amount of cash, or of theft or loss.

We decided to take the plunge and remove cash as a payment method, thinking that we could reintroduce it even if it failed.

We never had to.

All the objections that we thought we'd encounter, all the business that we thought we'd lose out on, they all didn't materialise. What happened was we achieved great improvements in risk, efficiency, and productivity instead.

Find out what assumptions you're running on, and test to see if they're valid. It could save you tonnes of time and resources when you're trying to increase business efficiency.

Simplify

Once you've removed all the tasks that aren't necessary or are distracting your business from its goals, you have to now simplify whatever tasks that are left.

Simplification is an art. A lot of times, things get more complex over time. I'm sure you've experienced a brand new computer being super-fast, but slows down considerably over time. That's when you have to start cleaning up your computer and removing unnecessary junk.

Left unchecked, business processes are the same. You'll need to simplify and streamline processes so that they can run optimally. You will know when your process is simple when they fulfil the following criteria:

- Easy to find;
- Easy to understand;
- Easy to execute; and
- Efficient.

What is the alternative? It is to have a business function that is chaotic. Nobody knows the boundaries because they are blurry. Everyone spends a lot of time on just trying to find out who needs to do what and when.

Here are some steps that you can follow in order to simplify your processes so that you can increase business efficiency.

- **Get organised**

  The way to start is to clean up all the clutter and organise everything clearly. Take a look at your processes and have everything mapped out. See if there are convoluted processes or if processes needed unnecessary steps.

  A good example is asking for approval. For example, perhaps you can state that all expense claims for amounts less than $10 can be automatically approved. This will not only save time for your employee but for your administration department.

  In addition, make sure ownership is clear for every step of your processes. Never put a team or have multiple owners for any step. This will ensure clear ownership and responsibilities, as well as reduce confusion.

- **Match the right task with the right talent**

  Your processes might be perfectly structured but might still be suboptimal because of the people who are working on them.

  Maybe you don't have the right talent in your company because your hiring processes are flawed.

  Maybe you have the right talent but they aren't at their full potential because they aren't getting the right training, or your leadership isn't optimal.

  Whatever the case, you need to fix it in order to increase business efficiency. Get the right people working on the right tasks and you'll see an immediate improvement.

- **Evaluate processes regularly**

  Processes aren't fixed in stone. In fact, as a business scales up, it is normal to find that it outgrows previous processes. Therefore, you need to regularly review processes to see if they can still meet their objectives efficiently.

  A lot of companies have embraced the policy of "unlimited leave days". This means that leave days don't have to be tracked. This makes sense because, after all, the organisation doesn't really care about how many days the employee is around. Instead, the employee is appraised based on how well he or she performs. This means that if the employee is away for half of the year, he or she likely won't have the performance to fulfil their job scope and will be terminated anyways.

  Therefore, being intentional and evaluating your processes for the intent that you want can greatly simplify things.

  Remember also that while systems may be led by you, processes are run by your team members. Get their feedback about processes regularly and understand if any processes are broken or need improvement or deeper investigation. This empowers the people handling these tasks and shows them that they can be recognised for finding more efficient and less expensive methods of completing their tasks.

- **Promote better communication**

  Good communication is essential for good teamwork. If you can't communicate well, you can't increase business efficiency.

  If you're doing things by yourself, communication is pretty easy— hopefully! After all, you only have to make sure that you understand what and why you're doing things. However, introduce one more person to work with and it gets much more difficult. Introduce a team, much less a large team, and it becomes exponentially difficult.

  This all has got to do with the difficulties of communicating. There are many ways to improving this, or at least, making it no more difficult than it has to be.

  The first thing to do is to ensure that everyone on the team shares the same values and believes in the company's vision. If there is a fundamental misalignment in values or vision, then it makes communications even more difficult.

  As an extreme example, if you are running a steakhouse, then perhaps hiring a vegan might not be the best fit for your team. You have to understand that communicating intentions and decisions are probably more difficult when there is a fundamental conflict in an individual's way of living and the business's vision.

  In more everyday situations, we have to ensure that our hires match the values and vision that our companies have.

  Secondly, invest time and effort into creating communication systems. This doesn't mean software systems. It just means having a standardised way of communications.

  Examples:
  - Only having meetings with clear agendas and objectives;
  - Ensuring meetings have a facilitator, who also ensures that meetings do not overrun;
  - Having guidelines on how projects are detailed so that there's a low chance of misunderstanding or miscommunication;

- Having a meeting cadence for regular communications upstream and downstream
- Using common file naming conventions—e.g. (company name) (document type)(date), which results in ABC_Pte_Ltd_ Proposal_051420—as this removes the mess of having many individual naming conventions in your company, resulting in people being able to find and identify files easier;
- Use common file repositories, like a shared drive or cloud storage.

If need be, you should invest in communication software that promotes the right kind of communication, such as chat software or project management software.

Software can potentially help increase business efficiency; but be careful of how you go about doing it: software should always be seen as a tool, not a solution.

Super Scaler Pro Tip: Don't purchase software with the intent for it to be a solution to solve your problems. It's common to think that software will be a magical solution to our business problems—they will not be. Always try to fix problems manually or in the non-scalable, tedious way first. Only after that should you consider investing in software that enhances your current working methods.

Automate

For me, automation is the most fun part of the ARSAD Funnel. Personally, I don't like doing manual and time-consuming tasks, especially if they happen on a recurring basis. These sorts of tasks are perfect to be automated using technology. Sometimes maybe the activity can't be automated easily, but you can automate the decision process or the trigger for the activity.

The key is to break up the processes and find the easiest parts to automate. These are your "low-hanging fruit", so always start with them first.

Here's a rule of thumb: If what you're doing is a step-by-step task, then you, as the business owner, probably should not be doing it. This was how work was like in the industrialisation age, and things are pretty different today. Automate any process-oriented tasks that you have on your plate, and free yourself up so that you can concentrate on high-value activities.

You don't even have to be an automation expert. Google for more information about basic processes that you'd like to automate. For example, you can try:

- How to automate report generation in Excel;
- How to automate PowerPoint slide creation;
- How to automate logins to a website;
- How to automate a file download.

When you get bigger, you can even hire developers to help you with larger-scale automation projects. These can really help increase business efficiency dramatically!

In Vodien, one of our core functions was customer support. To augment the manpower that we had supporting this function, we built an automated troubleshooting wizard. This helped our customer support officers by automating the process of troubleshooting and identifying common faults with customer accounts. It also greatly reduced the time it took to handle customer requests. Not only that, it greatly reduced human errors, and improved customer satisfaction.

Delegate

The very last component of the ARSAD Funnel is Delegate.

Efficiency is obtained by having the right people do the right tasks. You can't increase business efficiency if the wrong people are working on the wrong tasks or suboptimal tasks. This also applies to you.

Delegation should be a key consideration for anybody in your organisation. If someone else can do your job better, delegate the task to them. This comes with sacrifice too. In the scaling up of a company, we have to give up tasks that we enjoy but may not be best for the company.

Again, the story of Ben Francis, Gymshark's founder, comes to mind. Initially, he took on the role of CEO and scaling the company because he had to. It was only after the time was right that he stepped down and hired a better person to be CEO. Ben Francis then became the Chief Product Officer, finally returning to growing the product, which was an area that he enjoyed and was truly passionate about.

I loved programming, though I wasn't the best programmer around. When I was growing Vodien, I knew that I had to give up programming to my more capable team members so that I could focus on the more important things in running the business.

Sometimes, we have to give up what we like, in order for the business to scale up. And we have to bear in mind that giving up tasks doesn't reflect badly on ourselves. I used to think that it was irresponsible for me to give my work to others, but the reality is very much the opposite!

I grew up in a family that valued hard work and grit. For a long time, I had trouble letting go of tasks, because I felt that it was a sign of laziness if I "gave away" my work and got someone to work on it instead.

In fact, in the early years of starting Vodien with my co-founder, the two of us would handle and do everything that was necessary—accounting, marketing, finance, sales, product, research and development, literally everything!

Naturally, when the business grew, I faced huge demands on my time and attention that I couldn't cope with. I had big trouble wrapping my head around letting go of my tasks. Eventually, I was forced to do it, and gradually accepted the fact that it was the more efficient and responsible thing to do.

That was a big turning point and a major revelation to me. That was when I realised that my responsibility as CEO wasn't to be busy. My responsibility was to grow the company, and I couldn't do it if I was bogged down by doing day-to-day tasks.

This is especially true of your leadership team, not just the CEO. If any high-level executive is actually spending their time designing graphics or writing copy or anything executional, then your business is not utilising your manpower well.

If you find that you are the only one able to do the work, then you are the bottleneck in your company.

You should immediately look at hiring or developing a system around that task so that you can have that functionality handled by someone else in the company.

When you are able to find ways to delegate tasks, you will have the time and attention to focus on the higher-impact tasks. As a result, your organisation will come out even stronger.

Increase Business Efficiency

The way to increase business efficiency is not by ad hoc or one-time tricks and tactics. The focus on increasing productivity and efficiency in a systematic manner is fundamental to the successful transformation of your business operations.

Chapter 24

COMPOUNDING GROWTH

Question: What do you need to do in order to scale your business up?

You have to take big, broad, sweeping actions, right? Go big or go home. Take no prisoners. Burn the ships and crush it in every area. Come up with a new, revolutionary idea or strategy that has never been used before.

Actually, no. In fact, if you have a go big or go home mentality, there's a good chance that you'll go home.

See, here's the thing. Trying to make big, sweeping changes can feel incredibly overwhelming. You encounter a lot of resistance when you try to change too many things at one time. Many times, the resistance is so strong that you give up before you make any real progress.

So what is the solution?

Small, incremental improvements. Instead of shooting for 100% gains, shoot for 1% gains. In his book *Atomic Habits*, James Clear says:

> *"...improving by 1% isn't particularly notable— sometimes it isn't even noticeable—but it can be far more meaningful, especially in the long run. The difference a tiny improvement can make over time is astounding. Here's how the math works out: if you can get 1% better each day for one year, you'll end*

> up thirty-seven times better by the time you're done. Conversely, if you get 1% worse each day for one year, you'll decline nearly down to zero. What starts as a small win or a minor setback accumulates into something much more."

The secret to scaling your business is to focus on making small, almost imperceptible improvements. Don't try to make enormous changes. Consistent small changes produce more significant results in the long run than the occasional big change.

There's a common saying that you should shoot for the moon because even if you miss it, you'll still land among the stars. This is good advice, but most people interpret this to mean that you need to take huge actions if you want to achieve your dreams. The reality is that the key to reaching the "moon" is to aim just a little bit higher every day. Pretty soon, you'll find yourself flying higher than you've ever dreamed possible.

Look at almost any successful company and you'll see a history of incremental improvements that build upon each other. Apple, Google, Amazon, Facebook—they all rely heavily on constant incremental improvements to keep them ahead of the competition. Occasionally these companies release a new, big product, but even these big products tend to be improvements of other products. First, Apple released the iPod. They improved the iPod so that it could hold photos and have a touch screen. Eventually, these improvements led to the iPhone, which changed the world.

From Perennial Loser to Olympic Winner

In 2002, David Brailsford became the coach of the British national cycling team. Up to that point, the team had performed terribly, earning just a single Olympic gold medal in the past seventy-six years.

Two years after, they won two gold medals in the 2004 Olympics. In the 2008 Olympics in Beijing, the team won a staggering eight gold medals, and they repeated their performance again in the 2012 Olympics in London. Between 2002 to 2013, members of the British cycling team won a whopping fifty-nine world championships.

How did Brailsford engineer such an incredible turnaround?

It might surprise people, but there were no big, incredible breakthroughs. Instead, Brailsford focused on making small, incremental improvements. As he said in an interview with Eben Harrell for the Harvard Business Review:

> *"To give you a bit of background, when we first started out, the top of the Olympic podium seemed like a very long way away. Aiming for gold was too daunting. As an MBA, I had become fascinated with Kaizen and other process-improvement techniques. It struck me that we should think small, not big, and adopt a philosophy of continuous improvement through the aggregation of marginal gains. Forget about perfection; focus on progression, and compound the improvements."*

When Brailsford thought about trying to go from constantly losing to winning gold medals, he felt overwhelmed. So he put all his energy into incrementally improving. He painted team trucks white so that they could more easily spot dust that would interfere with finely tuned bikes. He rubbed alcohol onto the bike tires to improve their grip. He tested various muscle gels until he found one that enabled the riders to recover more quickly.

By themselves, none of these actions led to gold medals. But when you combine them all together, the total improvement was remarkable.

A 1% improvement every day leads to a 37x gain by the end of the year. Because of compounding, the gains aren't linear. Over time, the results get larger and larger.

So how can you implement the concept of incremental improvement in your business?

Get Everyone On Board

To really tap into the power of incremental improvement, you need to get everyone on board. See, here's the thing. In the beginning, the improvements don't produce much in terms of measurable results. Remember, we're talking about 1% improvements. It's hard to get excited about improvements that small if you don't have the big picture in view.

If your team members or management can't understand the compounding value of these small gains, they'll quickly grow impatient and start demanding bigger actions. They'll insist that you completely redesign the website or implement a new marketing strategy or come up with a new product to sell.

Again, to quote David Brailsford (Harrell):

> *"One caveat is that the whole marginal gains approach doesn't work if only half the team buy in. In that case, the search for small improvements will cause resentment. If everyone is committed, in my experience, it removes the fear of being singled out— there's mutual accountability, which is the basis of great teamwork."*

Everyone needs to understand that big results take time and commitment. If you jump from one growth "hack" to another, you won't make much progress at all. In fact, you may even find yourself going backwards. The first step in making incremental improvements is taking the time to ensure that everyone is on board with the process and knows what to expect.

Identify Your Most Important KPIs

Knowing your Key Performance Indicators (KPIs) allows you to evaluate whether your improvements are making a significant difference for your business. For example, say you are able to increase the percentage of people who sign up for a free trial of your product by 1%. While that certainly is a good thing, it won't help you much if hardly anyone converts from the free trial to a paid monthly subscription.

When you know your KPIs, you can focus your efforts on making improvements in the most critical areas of your business. Take the time to dig into your analytics and figure out which metrics are the most important. Do you need to focus on new leads generated every month? Monthly active users of your app? Reducing your churn rate?

Before you start making incremental improvements, identify the areas where those improvements will have the biggest impact.

Identify Key Processes

Each of your KPIs contains key processes that contribute to that specific indicator. For example, say that customer acquisition is a KPI for your business. What processes are involved in acquiring new customers? Maybe you run ads on Facebook. Maybe you send cold emails to potential prospects. Maybe you attend industry events.

Identify your key processes and each of the steps involved in those processes. Once you've identified all of the steps involved, you can strategically begin seeking to improve your performance at each step.

If you send cold emails, you can work on increasing your open rate and CTR (Click-Through Rate). If you run Facebook ads, you can focus on increasing the CTR and decreasing your cost per lead. You get the point. The more granular you can get when breaking down your processes, the more opportunities for improvement you'll have.

Experiment Constantly

Experiments are critical if you want to get marginal gains in your business. If you don't experiment, you won't know which actions will bring about improvements. However, there is a caveat to this statement. You need to have a structured testing process when it comes to running experiments. In other words, you need to run a test, evaluate and document the results, and then implement changes if appropriate. Then you can move onto the next test, and so on.

If you randomly run a bunch of tests at once, you'll have a hard time determining which experiment produced which results. For example, say you're trying to improve the email opt-in rate of a landing page. If you test multiple headlines, calls to action, and images at the same time, you won't know which items produced the best results. Test one element at a time. If it leads to improvements, implement the change and then move on to the next test.

Ultimately, all your changes need to be data-driven. Don't trust your gut. Only make changes when the data backs it up.

Amazon understands the power of systematically experimenting and then making small changes based on those experiments. As New York Times-bestselling author Chris DeRose told *Investor's Business Daily* (Tsuruoka):

> "As Amazon pursues growth through small experiments, they have tried to use data to trump intuition. The company culture embraces experimentation and Bezos recently said at a shareholder meeting that 99% of all innovations at Amazon are incremental. The company relies on 'Testing in Production', or TiP, methods such as A/B testing and ramped deployment. By showing user group 'A' a different version of a Web page than group 'B', the company can measure how long they stay on the site, how much they spend, etc."

When you take this systematic approach to experiments and tests, you eventually end up with big results.

Imagine if you had looked at the analytics of your e-commerce store and found that once a product had at least one review on the page, the sales of that product will be at least double your store's average performance.

What would you do in that case?

Most entrepreneurs will obviously jump at the opportunity. I would bet that they would try to find ways of increasing the number of product reviews that people would leave. Maybe they'd put in an email asking their customers for a review after three days of receiving their product. Maybe they'd even incentivise customers by offering them a chance at entering a lucky draw, or even membership points, if they leave a review.

Whatever it is, it's a simple but targeted change. And it results in a massive performance boost. If this was done for all your e-commerce store's product pages, it could easily mean an increase of sales of at least 10% across the board, all with just one change that typically only has a one-time cost of implementation.

Automate Processes

Automating time-intensive, tedious processes can help you make significant improvements in your business. The more you can automate low value activities, the more you can focus on tasks that actually move the needle for you.

For example, say you send twenty emails every day that are similar in format and structure. Each email only takes you one minute to send, which doesn't seem like much. But every day, you're spending twenty minutes on these emails, which adds up to a hundred minutes per week and 86.66 hours per year! If you can automate these emails in any way, you can save yourself a huge amount of time over the course of a year.

Look at your business and try to identify seemingly small, tedious tasks that are done regularly. This can include things like copying information between documents, getting sign-offs from multiple people on documents, organising digital information, etc. These kinds of tasks are perfect candidates for automation.

Tools like Zapier (Zapier.com) and IFTTT (IFTTT.com) make it really easy to automate tasks. They allow you to connect apps that don't normally "talk" to each other and automatically perform actions in those apps. So, for example, if you want to update a Google Sheet every time you get a new order in your Shopify store, you can easily do that with these tools.

Create Powerful Systems

When seeking to improve your business, you may be tempted to focus on specific goals. Maybe you want to make a hundred new sales this year or reduce product returns by 25%. And while goals can certainly be helpful in providing you with direction, creating powerful systems can be even more effective.

A system is simply a series of actions you take that constantly move you toward your desired objective. Instead of focusing on making a hundred new sales, create a series of actions that will help you constantly increase sales.

Your sales system could include:

- Making five cold calls every morning;
- Following up with five potential prospects every week;
- Running four online webinars each month.

To create your systems, identify the actions that will always push you toward your desired outcome. Then perform those actions on a consistent basis. Instead of focusing only on the goal, focus on the process. When you embrace the process instead of the goal, you don't get discouraged when you don't see immediate results.

Small Improvements, Big Results

In his book *The Slight Edge*, Jeff Olson writes:

> *"Success is the progressive realisation of a worthy ideal. 'Progressive' means success is a process, not a destination. It's something you experience gradually, over time. Failure is just as gradual. In fact, the difference between success and failure is so subtle, you can't even see it or recognise it during the process. And here's how real success is built: by the time you get the feedback, the real work's already done."*

If you want to scale your business and be successful, incremental improvement is the key. Don't look for the special one hack or trick that will bring you huge amounts of growth. Rather, look for a hundred small hacks that will grow your business just a little bit.

The good news is, the more committed you are to making these small improvements, the faster you can grow your company. Sean Ellis, the founder of GrowthHackers, talked about how he used rapid experimentation to dramatically grow his company:

> *"We grew from 90,000 MAU [monthly active users] to 152,000 MAU in about eleven weeks without spending a dollar on advertising or increasing the size of our growth team. The only thing that changed was the velocity of our experimentation. We achieved that velocity improvement by adopting the high tempo testing framework to help us prioritise and close the loop on the growth experiments that we thought would move the needle."*

I think it's important to note that they didn't spend any money on advertising to achieve that rapid growth. Rather, they focused intensely on making small improvements as rapidly as possible. As you can see, the results were extraordinary.

Are you ready to start scaling your business and achieve results you never thought possible? Then begin focusing relentlessly on making incremental improvements on a consistent basis. Be patient. You probably won't see impressive results immediately, but they'll come. And when they do, you'll be amazed.

At the end of the day, just realise that massive success DOES NOT require massive action. What is required—and is more sustainable— is making tiny improvements on a daily basis over a really long period of time.

Get More Super Scaling Resources

To help you with Super Scaling your business, I've created an online page just for you to access exclusive tools and resources. Scan the QR code on the left or go to:

SuperScaling.com/resources

TAKE ACTION NOW

Congratulations! You've reached the end of the book. How do you feel right now? A little overwhelmed? Excited at the possibilities?

Now that you've seen how the 5E Scale Engine works, you can see how powerful it is for building the business that you want. The lessons that I shared took me seventeen years to painfully experience and learn.

I want to share them with you because these lessons will prevent you from making numerous mistakes and save you much precious time. All these were real-life lessons and nothing is fiction.

Super scaling is a long-term process. Super scaling a business is never about just getting more customers. I hope you now realise that it's never about the latest Facebook advertising hack or the next trick that would be trending. Scaling is not going to happen overnight, but by focusing on the right things, it can enable you to really structure your business to scale up properly.

Remember, your business isn't supposed to be a stressful, eighty-hour-per-week job. It's a vehicle for you to:

- Create the kind of impact that you'd like to see;
- Generate wealth from the value you create;
- Give you time freedom.

The key is to do it systematically so that we can get to the results that we want. Using the 5E Scale Engine, most of the problems that most entrepreneurs get themselves into can be solved.

However, besides just knowledge, we really require three main things in order to make lasting transformational changes.

Mindset

Knowing what to do is one thing, but we oftentimes hold ourselves back or sabotage ourselves because our mindset controls us subconsciously. Changing our mindset requires time and effort. It's made more difficult because we don't know what we don't know.

Accountability

Again, knowing what to do isn't enough. We need to actually do it. The motivation that's needed to take action has two aspects to it: intrinsic motivation and extrinsic motivation.

Wanting to do it is one thing, but having an extrinsic motivational factor makes it even more powerful. For example, if you want to work out regularly, this could be a workout buddy or a personal trainer.

For business, it's the same thing. Having an accountability buddy forces us to focus on and stick to the tasks that really moves the needle.

Community

I found that I made a lot of mistakes the hard way when I was growing Vodien. I also spent a lot of time experimenting and trying out things for myself, because I didn't know anyone else who was in business that I could reach out to. That's why having a trusted peer that you can confide in and get advice from can be so beneficial.

I've found that the best way to develop these points in a structured manner is to have a trusted network of peers.

THE POWER OF A
NETWORK OF PEERS

When my co-founder and I founded Vodien, we were 100% bootstrapped, meaning that we didn't raise any external investments. The initial start-up capital wasn't much, so we funded it ourselves and grew it as best as we could. Neither of us knew how anything worked, but somehow, we managed to figure it out as we went along.

As we grew and matured into an organisation, we started having proper responsibilities and structures. There was no way we could have continued growing if we didn't. It was like a child growing to be a teenager and having to figure out puberty and all the changes that came with it—your voice breaking, height increasing, and limbs growing faster than you know how to control.

Unlike being a teenager, there wasn't much of a circle of close business friends that my co-founder and I had. We had business associates that we knew but we were pretty much on our own.

Our families and friends weren't the best people who might help us. They could listen and lend an ear for sure, but they couldn't give us the guidance nor advice nor perspective that we needed. Thankfully, both of us had a tremendous work ethic and we simply persevered through everything.

I loved what I was doing, but I was doing this in a very isolated way. Later, when I spoke to more entrepreneurs, I realised that it was a common situation for entrepreneurs to be in. The very nature of running businesses puts us in a position where we very commonly feel a sense of loneliness and isolation. We, as entrepreneurs, typically lack trusted peers that we can exchange information with.

This is usually combined with long hours, lots of sacrifices of personal/ social activities, and a serious focus on work. It's no wonder that this lack of community results in a degradation in mental health, personal performance, and organisational excellence.

I know entrepreneurs have tried to solve it before with business networks and societies. However, the danger of not having a tightly-knit group with a clear focus is that the network typically deviates very quickly. The network either becomes highly transactional, where members start soliciting business from other members, or becomes a social club where members congregate for entertainment activities instead of focusing on business scaling.

I believe that just like any interest group or hobby, entrepreneurs who have a focus on scaling up will benefit from a trusted network of like-minded peers, where the community element can help everyone inside run more successful businesses.

In Napoleon Hill's *Think and Grow Rich*, he describes a mastermind group as:

> *"The coordination of knowledge and effort of two or more people, who work toward a definite purpose, in the spirit of harmony."*

Hill is right. This is what good teamwork is and is the reason why some teams can be high-performing while others have lacklustre performance. The difference is the clarity of purpose and the harmony in terms of values and core beliefs of the individuals. The common purpose that binds people together in a network or community is also what makes it powerful.

I run a network like this for entrepreneurs, where everyone is clear on the mission: scaling up their businesses. I concentrate on providing the four main things that entrepreneurs need to break through and reach the next level: focus, accountability, knowledge, and community.

We meet regularly to reflect, listen, share, and support each other through our professional growth. Here are four ways that a community of peers can help you to sharpen your entrepreneurial skill set and become a better leader.

Tackle the Toughest Challenges of Leadership

Running a business is not easy. I've found that the path of entrepreneurship is a lonely one. Oftentimes, our friends and family won't be able to help. We need to surround ourselves with peers who understand what we're going through. We need peers who can validate us and ask us the tough questions that others won't ask.

Having such a safe space where we are amongst peers is crucial. This allows us to explore our doubts, struggles, and frustrations, and to get support and ideas from peers who are also on the same journey.

Doing things alone can be a huge sap on our energy. Having this support from a community gives us the energy and vigour to continue to maximise our impact and achieve our business goals.

An Education You Can't Get in a Classroom

Building a successful business requires having the right mindset and focus, hiring and growing a solid team, managing finances, and optimising operations. The practical aspects of these topics can be very different from the theoretical aspects. Taking a class at school can give us foundational knowledge, but that's the extent of their usefulness. These classes aren't typically the best way to get answers when we're faced with executional obstacles.

When we connect with entrepreneur peers, it allows powerful questions to be raised around critical business functions, and answers to be developed together. The perspective from knowledgeable peers can also help us avoid our weaknesses and double down on our strengths.

When we hear the different views of other trusted peers, it allows us to see issues that we would have been otherwise been unaware of. We don't have to agree with their assessments. The key is that it gives us a better understanding of how we can improve our approach and execution, and more importantly, avoid being blindsided by things that we would have missed.

Sharing Resources

Every entrepreneur does what they do because they have found a problem that they want to fix, or an inefficiency that can be improved, or an opportunity in the market. The issue is that we are typically only strong in a certain domain. These skill sets, knowledge, and networks that we know can be very powerful if we share them with trusted peers who otherwise would not have access to them.

Finding peers with whom we can share our resources with will allow everyone to make a lot more happen—be it introductions to contacts, business opportunities, or expertise in a specific domain.

Having Accountability and Focus

As entrepreneurs, it's never the case that we don't have anything to do. We are always busy. The danger is being busy for the sake of being busy and not focusing on the things that will really move the needle in your business.

Therefore, it becomes apparent that one of the major obstacles to success is not having the right focus and accountability. Having a close community solves this. Everyone keeps everyone accountable to his or her goals. In addition, we can see if someone isn't being focused enough in his or her goals.

Surround yourself with the people who will share educational insights, support each other, and work with each other to achieve business goals.

Join A Community of Entrepreneurs

I've created an online community of entrepreneurs just for this purpose. It's entirely free to join, but I'm strict on who gets to join (I only accept entrepreneurs and business owners). To join, just head here:

SuperScaling.com/go/group

START SUPER SCALING

I hope that you use this book and the resources that I have made available as your launch pad. The key is to transform your business and scale up.

As a buyer of the book, I'm making available to you some of the tools and resources that I've used to Super Scale my business. Just pop over to this page to access them:

SuperScaling.com/resources

Changes that you make to yourself and your business will start affecting everybody, from your team, customers, family, and life.

I've experienced it for myself and seen it in the entrepreneurs that I coach. I hope to see it in you too, so please let me know your results. Reach out to me on social media, and join the Super Scalers group as well:

SuperScaling.com/go/group/

When I was running Vodien, I would have loved to have a book like this that could guide me to what was necessary for scaling up. My mission is to have entrepreneurs all over the world be able to read and learn from this book, just like how you've benefitted.

If this book has given you value, please consider leaving a review that might help another entrepreneur, and have this book reach more people around the world.

To make it easier, I've created a page here:

SuperScaling.com/review

See you real soon,
Alvin Poh

BIBLIOGRAPHY

Adams, Scott. "Goals vs. Systems." *Scott Adams Says,* 18 Nov. 2013, https://www.scottadamssays.com/2013/11/18/goals-vs-systems/. Accessed 25 February 2021.

Adams, Scott. *How to Fail at Almost Everything and Still Win Big: Kind of the Story of My Life.* Portfolio, 2013.

Bernazzani, Sophia. "The Beginner's Guide to Building a Customer Loyalty Program." HubSpot, 25 Nov. 2019, https://blog.hubspot.com/service/customer-loyalty-program. Accessed 13 October 2020.

Chambers, Sarah. "From Ideas to Action: 6 Creative Ways to Show Customers You Care." *Shopify Blog,* 31 May 2019, https://www.shopify.com/blog/thank-your-customers. Accessed 5 January 2021.

Ciotti, Gregory. "10 Unforgettable Customer Service Stories." *HelpScout,* 15 Sep. 2020, https://www.helpscout.com/10-customer-service-stories/. Accessed 21 December 2020.

Clear, James. *Atomic Habits: An Easy & Proven Way to Build Good Habits and Break Bad Ones.* Avery, 2018.

Danziger, Pamela. "Amazon's Customer Loyalty Is Astounding." *Forbes,* 10 Jan. 2018, https://www.forbes.com/sites/pamdanziger/2018/01/10/amazons-customer-loyalty-is-astounding/. Accessed 19 November 2020.

Davies, Sam Thomas. *Directives: A Brief Guide on What to Do from The Best in The World.* Self-published.

Ellis, Sean. "High Tempo Testing Revives GrowthHackers.com Growth." *GrowthHackers,* https://growthhackers.com/growth-studies/high-tempo-testing-revives-growthhackers-com-growth. Accessed 20 February 2021.

Fabbioni, Alessia. "Best of Zappos Customer Service Stories." *Medium,* 7 May 2019, https://medium.com/@alessiafabbioni/best-of-zappos-customer-service-stories-543606d76637. Accessed 26 July 2020.

Gallo, Amy. "The Value of Keeping the Right Customers." *Harvard Business Review,* 29 Oct. 2014, https://hbr.org/2014/10/the-value-of-keeping-the-right-customers. Accessed 3 December 2020.

Haden, Jeff. "20 Years Ago, Jeff Bezos Said This 1 Thing Separates People Who Achieve Lasting Success From Those Who Don't." *Inc.,* 6 Nov. 2017, https://www.inc.com/jeff-haden/20-years-ago-jeff-bezos-said-this-1-thing-separates-people-who-achieve-lasting-success-from-those-who-dont.html. Accessed 22 January 2021.

Harrell, Eben. "How 1% Performance Improvements Led to Olympic Gold." *Harvard Business Review,* 30 Oct. 2015, https://hbr.org/2015/10/how-1-performance-improvements-led-to-olympic-gold. Accessed 25 February 2021.

Hill, Napoleon. *Think and Grow Rich.* Sound Wisdom, 2017.

Hull, Patrick. "Don't Get Lazy About Your Client Relationships." *Forbes,* 6 Dec. 2013, https://www.forbes.com/sites/patrickhull/2013/12/06/tools-for-entrepreneurs-to-retain-clients/. Accessed 18 October 2020.

Liang, Victor. *The Secret of All Success and Riches: Discovering the Secret of Success and Achieving Your Personal Dreams and Desires.* iUniverse, 2014.

Motista. "Leveraging the Value of Emotional Connection for Retailers." *Motista,* 27 Sep. 2019, https://www.motista.com/resource/leveraging-value-emotional-connection-retailers01. Accessed 2 October 2020.

Nielson. "Global Trust in Advertising and Brand." 4 Jul. 2012, https://www.nielsen.com/us/en/insights/report/2012/global-trust-in-advertising-and-brand-messages-2/. Accessed 5 January 2021.

Olson, Jeff. *The Slight Edge: Turning Simple Disciplines into Massive Success and Happiness.* Greenleaf Book Group Press, 2013.

Reichheld, Fred. "Prescription for Cutting Costs." *Bain & Company,* 1 Sep. 2001, https://media.bain.com/Images/BB_Prescription_cutting_costs.pdf. Accessed 5 September 2020.

Saleh, Khalid. "Customer Acquisition Vs. Retention Costs—Statistics And Trends." *Invesp,* 19 Nov. 2019, https://www.invespcro.com/blog/customer-acquisition-retention/. Accessed 28 August 2020.

Tsuruoka, Doug. "Amazon Secret Weapon Is Its Experimental Culture." *Investor's Business Daily,* 25 Jun. 2013, https://www.investors.com/news/ technology/amzn-experiments-learns-from-its-mistakes/.   Accessed   4 January 2021.